Making College Pay

Making College Pay

An Economist Explains How to Make a
Smart Bet on Higher Education

BETH AKERS

Currency
New York

Published in the United States by Currency, an imprint of Random House,
a division of Penguin Random House LLC, New York.

CURRENCY and its colophon are trademarks of Penguin Random House LLC.

The chart on p. 71 is courtesy of Anthony P. Carnevale, Ban Cheah, and
Martin Van Der Werf, *The Economic Value of College Majors* (Washington, D.C.:
Georgetown University Center on Education and the Workforce, 2015).

Hardback ISBN 978-0-593-23853-0
Ebook ISBN 978-0-593-23854-7

Printed in Canada on acid-free paper

crownpublishing.com

2 4 6 8 9 7 5 3 1

First Edition

*For my son, who I expect will be routinely rejecting all of my advice
out of hand by the time he's old enough to read this*

Contents

Preface

When I finished my college degree, a bachelor's in math and economics from the state university nearest to where I grew up, I headed straight to graduate school to start a PhD. Finishing a PhD and becoming a professor had been my dream since a few weeks into my first semester of an economics course as a freshman, when I fell in love with the discipline. I'd tailored almost every course and experience I'd had during those four years to making this goal come to fruition. I switched my first major from economics to math, which, illogically, provides the clearest pathway to a PhD in economics, and I picked my classes on the basis of the sole criterion of how well they would prepare me for graduate school in economics, which meant more math and less everything else. (This will come as no surprise to anyone who has had the distinct misfortune of having me on their team for any sort of trivia game.)

But once I got to graduate school, I quickly realized that I was woefully unprepared. My singular focus on preparing for graduate school admissions had left me relatively well equipped to solve math proofs and calculate a 15 percent tip in my head but it left me lacking the contextual knowledge—in history, humanities, current affairs—that would make a deep understanding of economics worthwhile. I was about two years into my PhD program when I decided I needed to step back and take some time to remind myself why economics mattered.

Then, in some bizarre and strange twist of fate, the opportunity of a lifetime fell into my lap. I was invited to spend a year at the White House working in the President's Council of Economic Advisers, the group of academic economists working within the Executive Office of the President to advise senior policy makers on all matters of economics. I joined the team in the summer of 2007. The George W. Bush administration was nearing the end of its term, so I expected that I'd have a pretty uneventful tenure. But then, out of nowhere, the mortgage crisis struck the US economy—and it struck hard. Needless to say, it was suddenly a very exciting time to be a young economist in the nation's capital.

Unbeknownst to most people, another crisis was looming that coincided with the one in the mortgage market. The tumult in the credit markets combined with a design flaw in the federal student loan program made it such that lenders wouldn't have been able or willing to make loans to students that fall. Credit had dried up, and without action, college students across the country would have been locked out of college for that fall semester, since lenders weren't going to be willing to make any loans to help students pay their tuition bills. I worked on a small team that implemented a policy patch, made possible by emergency legislation, to address the immediate problem. My understanding about public policy and "real-world" economics jumped from nil to "firsthand experience" in an absurdly short period of time. And I suddenly had the motivation, and knowledge, to be able to return to my PhD program and complete a dissertation on student debt.

After finishing my PhD, I failed to land the academic job of my dreams and instead was hired as a researcher at a think tank, the Brookings Institution. (This turned out to be my actual dream job, but I didn't know it at the time.) One of my responsibilities in that job was to answer the phone when reporters called and share my insights on the issue du jour. Oddly enough, precious few of these reporters were seeking comments for a big, splashy cover story on the economics of higher education. But after asking about whatever issue was making headlines that day, nearly every reporter, without fail, would end the call with the same curiosity: "So, is there a student loan crisis on the horizon?"

It was a question I didn't know how to answer. It wasn't that I *couldn't* answer, but rather that my understanding of the issue seemed at odds with the way that the general public and mainstream media were discussing it.

This was in 2012. At that point we were just three years removed from the peak of the financial crisis, which was widely understood to have been caused by irresponsible mortgage lending. It seemed to me that people were now looking askance at the student loan market, wondering whether the rise in student debt would drive us into the second wave of the Great Recession. On the surface, it was easy to see parallels between what had happened in the housing market and what had been happening in student lending. We'd seen a dramatic rise both in the amount students were borrowing and in the number of students who were borrowing.

But the defining characteristics of the student loan market were (and are) actually quite different from those of the mortgage market. Unlike with houses, most people aren't overpaying for college. That's because, despite the high price tags, the extra earnings afforded by a college degree tend to far outweigh the up-front cost.

In 2016, I had the opportunity to publish a book about my findings, *Game of Loans*, coauthored with Matthew Chingos. The book was warmly received by many but criticized by some: namely those who were unable or unwilling to relinquish the trusted narratives about college loans as an impediment to economic and social advancement for both individuals and the nation. The book aimed to lay out evidence that would allow policy makers to see the economics of higher education in a new light.

In effect, the book didn't go much beyond refuting the popular but incorrect narratives about student debt. Once that project was in the rearview mirror, I felt compelled to write another book: one that could help policy makers and academics understand the *real* problems in how higher education is financed in America—and in turn help them craft policy that would actually help those who need it the most. But in the process of writing that book, I realized that policy makers and academics weren't the ones who needed to hear what I had to say. They already had access to my work and to the work of many talented researchers and analysts who came before me. Instead, I realized, it was actually students and their families—those of you grappling with the tough decisions about how to pay for college—who could benefit most from my approach.

As a graduate student, I had needed to step away from the process of earning a degree in order to truly appreciate why economics mattered. Over a decade later, it was only in the process of trying to write a different book, one that you surely wouldn't have wanted to read, that I realized a new way in which economics matters. Economics is simply a lens—a way of looking at a problem. And I believe that examining the problem of how to pay for college—and how to make college pay for you—through that lens will empower you to make the best decisions possible.

Making College Pay

College Is Still Worth It

S tudent debt makes for frightening headlines and politics. Millennials being crushed by their payments, being forced to live in their parents' basements and failing to launch into adulthood: delaying home purchases, marriage, and having children. Professionals in their thirties and forties who find themselves with accruing balances on their loans despite making the required monthly payments. And perhaps the most frightening of all, retirees whose Social Security payments are being withheld to repay the student debts they weren't successful in repaying before retirement.

Collectively, the current outstanding balance of student loans in the United States is astronomical: over $1.6 trillion. The magnitude of that number has struck fear into the hearts of many Americans and continues to do so, as it is cited on a nearly daily basis on the pages of top newspapers. So too has the rising cost of college: a burdensome, if not financially crippling, expense for students and families across the socioeconomic spectrum.

Or at least, it seems that way, doesn't it? It seems that way because that is the story you're being told. Newspapers and the cable news shows have made a habit of telling the horror stories about student loans; after all, these are the stories that get the most eyeballs. But the reality is completely different. It's not that stories you're hearing in media are lies; it's simply that they are outliers. To see the full picture, we need to look past the horror stories experienced by the few and turn our focus to the success stories revealed by the data.

Understanding the Trade-Offs

I spent the first several years of my career researching the economics of higher education more broadly, in an attempt to reconcile this widely accepted narrative with the evidence. My work confirmed that both the cost of college and the amount of debt that students are taking on are accelerating. But also, student debt is a pretty powerful tool that can help people afford college who wouldn't otherwise be able to go. And it turns out that despite the scary price tag, college is, for the most part, worth it.

This notion that college is worth it is implicitly endorsed by policy makers, yet simultaneously rejected in our collective rhetoric around student debt. It's long been a national objective to put more and more students in and through college each year. We all know on some level, at least intuitively, that college is worth it. If it weren't, our nation wouldn't spend several tens of billions of dollars annually to encourage enrollment. If it weren't, politicians wouldn't be constantly trumpeting their plans to increase college enrollment rates, and policy makers, advocates, and practitioners wouldn't constantly be seeking new ways to get more and more people access to education after high school. If college didn't pay, it'd hardly be worthy of so much effort.

And yet while we all celebrate the promise of college as the path to upward mobility—the ticket to more productive and prosperous lives—there is a simultaneous outrage over the price tag and a belief that students who borrow to pay for their degrees have been victimized by the system. It is precisely the dissonance between these two simultaneously held views that has motivated me to learn more and help others better understand the economics of education after high school. It seems to me that it's necessary to reconcile these conflicting sentiments, at least individually, so that aspiring students and their families can make sound decisions about how much to spend and if, where, and when to enroll in college. And it almost goes without saying that without reconciling these conflicting notions we cannot craft policy that works toward the greater goal of improving the welfare of all Americans, but especially those who aren't born with a silver spoon in their mouth.

I am in my late thirties, which means that I'm beginning to have friends and acquaintances with children in college or getting close to it. I've had the distinct pleasure of being able to talk with many of these college-bound young adults as they explored the options for after high school. Something that has been quite striking to me during those exchanges is how the notion of financial trade-offs is so often absent from the decision-making process.

Recently I spoke with one young man who was considering several different options. He shared with me that he had managed to narrow down his list but was now somewhat torn between two academically similar colleges. The first would likely offer him a full academic scholarship, whereas he'd probably pay full freight at the other—about $100,000. He recognized that the first option was cheaper, of course. The problem, he told me, was that he really preferred the look of the campus at the second, more expensive one.

The mother, economist, and all-around cheapskate in me almost fainted at the thought that he'd throw away the opportunity to attend college on a full scholarship over a matter as trivial as the aesthetics of the campus. Yet I've had versions of this conversation repeatedly with different students facing different, seemingly obvious (to me, at least) trade-offs. These students often cite geographic preference, the competitiveness of sports teams, size of the student body, and availability of certain clubs or extracurricular activities when weighing their choices for where to enroll. And don't get me wrong, these are all reasonable factors to consider. But they seem to play an outsized role in the decision-making process relative to economic factors like up-front cost and the likely employment opportunities after graduation. These young people aren't ignorant, reckless, or naïve by nature. They are simply a product of a culture that has celebrated college-going as if it were a golden ticket. By overemphasizing romantic notions about finding "the perfect fit" (as though college were a pair of jeans, or a spouse), our culture tends to discourage aspiring students from being appropriately critical consumers when shopping for colleges.

My instinct in those moments is not to lecture (well, maybe a tiny bit) but simply to help these young people recognize the trade-offs they are making. I want them to appreciate that the joy of announcing on social media the name of the prestigious college they've chosen or playing frisbee on a beautiful campus quad every other weekend will be fleeting but that the financial implications of their choice will last decades. Of course, money isn't everything. But I want aspiring students to appreciate the economics inherent in the choices they are making.

This book is my attempt to impart all the advice I'd like to give those young people, while also offering a new way of thinking about the decision in front of you.

The Economics of College

To start, we need to define what we mean when we ask whether the price of tuition is "worth it." Using an economic lens, we can say that college is worth it if the boost in lifetime earnings afforded by a degree exceeds the cost (adjusting for inflation, interest payments on loans, and forgone earnings while enrolled). It's a simple and satisfying idea largely rooted in Nobel Prize–winning economist Gary Becker's notion of human capital: that education is merely, or at least largely, a process of skill accumulation and that the accompanying expense is either justified by the improved earnings opportunities that it affords in the future or not. In other words, college is worth it if paying for it leads to greater wealth from earnings in the long run.

The notion of college-going as a purely financial, even mathematical decision is largely at odds with the way that it is portrayed in popular culture: as an intellectually and socially enriching experience complete with Greek life, tailgating at homecoming games, and hours of philosophical pontificating over espresso with the supposedly infinitely available faculty. Colleges themselves often reinforce this perspective with their messaging. For example, Trinity College, a small liberal arts college in Hartford, Connecticut, states on its website that a degree from there will prepare you to be "a bold, independent thinker who leads a transformative life." Such a glorious notion. Leading a transformative life, you say? How much does that pay?

Trinity is an easy target with that lofty notion plastered on their mission statement. But it isn't exceptional in this way. Colleges and universities have sold us on the idea that having an immersive college career with all the bells and whistles of a five-star resort (the extracurricular activities, the beautiful quad, the luxurious campus amenities) is a magically transformative experience. And perhaps it is. But for the 90 percent of aspiring college students who report on surveys that their primary motivation for going to college is to earn more money or to advance in their career, all of this romanticism about college-going may be causing some to make decisions they'll later regret.

We're missing another important point about colleges behind the same smoke and mirrors. Colleges would like you to believe they are benevolent institutions. And in some sense, many are. Their explicit missions generally involve creating opportunity for their students and contributing to society in any number of ways. But in another sense, they are no different from the multitudes of other businesses that serve us in other aspects of our lives. They have balance sheets and bills to pay. They are businesses that will continue to exist only if they can create value for their customers.

I fear that our putting colleges on a pedestal has driven us to make decisions about college-going that don't serve our self-interest. We are often so flattered by our acceptance to a big-name college that we'll do whatever it takes to pay the bill. It's a mentality that stands in the way of aspiring students being able to make sound economic decisions.

To appreciate the absurdity of the dynamic, imagine if we celebrated our relationships with other service providers to the same extent. I really do like my accountant, but I never posted on my social media when they accepted me as a client. And I don't even own any swag with their brand emblazoned on it. The truth is, my allegiance to them is fickle. If they let me down or raise their prices, I'm off to look for a new accountant. We don't have this mentality with regard to higher education, but we ought to.

Further distorting the way we make decisions about college is the way our culture treats college enrollment as if it is a contest to be won. A certain class of graduating high school seniors have made a tradition of announcing on social media where they plan to enroll in college the following fall. "Decision Day" now happens on May 1 each spring. But this spectacle seemingly undermines the fact that college enrollment is not a prize to be won or a God-given right but a financial decision, and a tremendously high-stakes one.

My point isn't to ruin the fun of those who wish to rush a sorority, debate the works of the great philosophers, or celebrate an important milestone in their lives but instead to point out that we've been conditioned by society to divorce decisions regarding college enrollment from the underlying economics. And when facing the big decisions—like if and where to enroll, how much to pay, and how much to borrow—we need to treat college as we would any other financial decision: that is, by weighing the benefits against the costs.

Yes, college is expensive. The sticker price at many top institutions, more than $50,000 per year, would consume nearly 80 percent of the annual income of the median household in the United States. And borrowing to pay for college can leave graduates with debt loads that exceed the amount they will take home in their first year on the job. The typical graduate with student debt will complete their bachelor's degree owing almost $30,000, whereas 2019 data shows that on average, new graduates had annual earnings of approximately $50,000.

Those benchmarks are often used to argue that the cost of college places an undue burden on students and their families. But those comparisons reveal an inappropriate method of analysis. College degrees need to be paid for just once, while annual earnings and the wage premium paid to college graduates are collected for the duration of a worker's career. In essence, deeming the cost of college too high by comparing it to annual earnings makes the mistake, to use economics jargon, of comparing a "stock" (student debt) to a "flow" (annual income). For example, do we assess the affordability of a new home by comparing the total price tag to our salary? No. That's because we expect to benefit from the home for many years to come, whereas our salary needs to sustain us only for the year (taking into account some savings, of course). Instead, we compare the amortized cost of the home, in terms of monthly mortgage payments, to our monthly ability to pay. It'd be absurd to consider it any other way, and it's absurd that we seldom, if ever, consider the expense of college in the same way.

But when we use the correct sort of analysis—comparing the up-front cost of college to the additional earnings it'll likely yield over a lifetime—evidence from researchers paints a very clear picture. Study after study, across a variety of different methods, has indicated that college degrees, on average, are worth far more than their price tag.

For example, when researchers from the New York Federal Reserve Bank calculated the return on educational spending as if it were an investment in a stock or bond, they found that the average return on associate's and bachelor's degrees was 14 percent. By all measures, 14 percent is an abundant return—approximately double the return you'd expect in the stock market.

Other studies have measured the lifetime earnings of college graduates compared to those who didn't complete a degree. The crux of this strategy is to compare people who are similar in all characteristics that might affect earnings—socioeconomic class, geography, parents' level of educational attainment, et cetera—besides their educational attainment, to ensure that the results aren't capturing differences between those two groups other than their level of education.

The Center on Education and the Workforce at Georgetown University recently published a report of this nature showing that, on average, the additional earnings afforded by a degree over the course of forty years, minus the up-front cost of enrollment, amounted to nearly three-quarters of a million dollars for each student. Students attending liberal arts colleges fared even better, coming out almost $1 million ($918,000) ahead after forty years compared to what they would have earned without a degree. The cost they paid was high, but the benefit was even higher.

These findings are attributed not only to the higher salaries paid to college graduates (on average) compared to high school graduates but also to the fact that people with college degrees spend less time unemployed over their working life. The unemployment rates for workers with college degrees are consistently lower than the unemployment rates among their non-college-educated counterparts, and that gap generally widens during a downturn, as it is usually the case that workers with less education are the first to be let go when the economy begins to slow.

The promise of higher earnings over the course of forty years may be little consolation to those facing the terrifying prospect of a $50,000 tuition bill. But while those $50,000-per-year sticker prices at elite four-year intuitions often get a lot of attention in the public discourse on this issue, the typical college student pays just $85,000 for enrollment and living expenses, or about $21,000 a year, for their bachelor's degree. And the reality is that, thanks to financial aid programs, very few students actually pay the full $200,000 to earn a degree from the elite private colleges—and those who do can surely afford it. For example, despite the astonishingly high price tag of $71,785 per year at Columbia University, the average amount that was actually charged to students who received some aid was just $22,824.

Colleges, in economic parlance, are practicing a form of price discrimination: they list a high price tag to signal prestige and also to be able to collect that price from the wealthy students who can afford to pay it. Students who are less well-off receive aid from both the college, in the form of discounts, and the government, in the form of Pell Grants and tax credits. The result is that each student pays more or less what the college believes they can afford.

Moreover, while those astronomical price tags get attention for their shock value, they are not the norm. In fact, most students in the United States who go on to study after high school will enroll at a less expensive public institution. Among the students who enrolled in college in 2017, 74 percent were enrolled at public colleges, where the average annual cost in 2019–20, after grants and scholarships, was just over $15,000 (including living expenses): far from cheap, but also a fraction of that $50,000 number we tend to throw around. Of course, for most students, the up-front cost isn't the only factor; for those planning to finance part or all of their tuition through loans, it's important to also consider the cost of whatever debt they stand to take on. Luckily, this too turns out to be less expensive than we tend to believe.

What We Often Get Wrong
About Student Debt

Much of the concern about the cost of college is concentrated on students who borrow to pay for their degrees. Borrowing to pay for school does make it more expensive because of the interest payments and fees associated with borrowing. But even so, the return generally still far exceeds the cost. In part, that's because student loans are far cheaper than is generally perceived. The vast majority of student loans in the economy were originated by the federal government as Stafford Loans, which means they have below-market interest rates. Stafford loans currently have an interest rate of 2.75 percent, whereas credit cards are charging north of 12 percent. If you've bought a vehicle or financed (or refinanced) a home recently, you'll appreciate that these rates are well above those for auto and home loans. That's because those are "secured" loans, which are backed up by the property you are using them for. A lender can repossess your car if you stop making your payments. Repossessing your education (or credit card purchases) is much harder, hence the higher rates. The subsidy implicit in federal student lending programs means that students and their parents can actually use student loans to come out ahead. That's because student loans are essentially cheap cash.

For example, imagine a family with two adults earning a combined income of about $60,000 who aim to put their only child through a bachelor's degree program. The family could scrimp and save to pay the approximately $85,000 cost of attendance out of pocket, or they could finance a large portion of it using student loans. You might be inclined to think that it's best to pay as much in cash as you can afford. That's a reasonable assumption. But the truth is that it's almost always better to borrow as much as you can.

How can that be, when paying out of pocket means you'd face no interest payments? Because it also means that you won't be able to put the cash into other, perhaps more profitable investments, like the stock market. The way to think about the cost of using cash is not the up-front cost but what economists call the *opportunity cost* of the cash. In the case of the aforementioned household, the parents may have jobs that offer 401k retirement savings accounts. Because the effective rate of return on these sorts of accounts, which often include some sort of matching provisions, far exceeds the cost of borrowing through the student loan program, the financially savvy thing for this family to do is to pack away their cash into their retirement savings accounts until they've reached the limits and borrow to pay for school. Even families who have already maxed out their retirement savings contributions might find that they'd get a higher return on their cash by plugging it into an investment account, which will often yield returns higher than the cost of interest on a student loan or even paying. And paying down existing high-interest-rate debt, like credit cards, with that cash you save by borrowing for school also puts you ahead of the game. This probably explains why some of the most well-off households take on the highest levels of student debt. In 2016, students from households in the highest income quartile (those with income above $120,000) borrowed about $10,500 more than students from households in the lowest income quartile (those with incomes below $30,000).

The point is that borrowing to pay for college isn't always the last resort. In fact, it's the savvy thing to do for many families or individuals, even those with cash on hand. It's also important to realize that borrowers with student loan debt are often very well positioned financially to pay it back. While the popular media has frequently told horror stories about white-collar professionals struggling with loan repayment—like that of the orthodontist who managed to amass $1 million in student debt—the vast majority of borrowers have small balances and reasonable payments relative to their income.

The average millennial with a bachelor's degree and student debt would have an approximately $30,000 balance at graduation. By repaying those loans over the course of twenty years on a standard repayment plan, the borrower would make monthly payments of $181. By contrast, median earnings for that college-educated millennial would be $56,605. By this math a household with two college-educated earners would have an annual income of $113,210 and student loan payments of less than $400 per month, or just 4 percent of this family's pretax monthly income ($9,434). For perspective, the typical millennial household (including millennials without college degrees) is spending almost this much on monthly car payments ($329).

We needn't be so worried about those with high, scary balances, especially considering that the largest loan balances are held by people who pursued graduate or professional degrees and generally saw huge financial returns in the form of high earnings (e.g., doctors, lawyers). In 2017, the average annual income for millennials with master's and professional degrees was $74,480 and $89,006, respectively. That makes larger loan payments feasible—while still leaving much more discretionary income as well. With this in mind, you might be less surprised to learn that the borrowers with the most debt are the least likely to have financial difficulties with repayment, whereas the highest rates of default are seen among borrowers with less than $5,000 in debt, who often didn't complete a degree.

And for the portion of graduates who *are* struggling to pay back those loans, optional income-based repayment plans adjust payments to an affordable level (based on income, regional cost of living, and the size of the borrower's household) and forgive debt that is "unaffordable." When borrowers have a low enough level of earnings, their monthly payment due can even fall to zero. And better yet, balances that remain after ten or twenty years (depending on sector of employment) will be forgiven. While many borrowers do take advantage of the benefits of income-based student loan repayment, many more don't realize that they exist.

On paper, the economics of paying for college are simple. But in the real world, they can be anything but. That's largely because we've misdiagnosed the problem facing today's young people facing tough decisions about how to pay for college. We've pinned all of our concerns on the cost of college and developed solutions and strategies based on that diagnosis. For example, it has become popular among Democratic politicians to propose widespread forgiveness of student loans. That's an appealing intervention if you're holding some debt, but it's also inconsistent with the fact that many with student debt are among the highest earners in the economy. While loan forgiveness may allow a politician to claim "victory" over the student loan crisis, in reality it fails to solve the real problems.

The truth is that the cost isn't the problem. The problem, in economic terms, is actually the *risk* involved with the transaction. The challenge for young people considering college today is not the debt itself but how to balance and mitigate the financial risk inherent in borrowing. This distinction is not just semantics. Focusing on cost as the problem to solve has shifted our national dialogue about college toward solutions like socialized higher education or price controls, both of which would lead to a degradation of the quality of our higher education system. Solutions of this sort would leave our system of higher education with many of the classic problems that arise in public systems: underfunding, limited capacity resulting in rationing of access (probably to the exclusion of the neediest students), and ballooning expense paired with declines in innovation. It's also pushed students toward low-cost paths that offer false economy, like enrolling in community college with the intention of saving money before transferring to a university, only to end up not graduating and instead joining the workforce without any sort of credential.

Paying for and enrolling in colleges requires trade-offs. The money and time you spend on college can't be simultaneously spent on something else. And by choosing one college or major you're *not* choosing another. These decisions mean picking one thing over the other. Different paths will have different up-front costs, different likely payoffs, and different levels of inherent risk. In choosing one path over another, aspiring students and their families should know what they are signing up for relative to what they are forgoing. Only by making decisions with these factors in mind can aspiring students make the choice they are least likely to regret.

In the chapters that follow, I'll make the case that our biggest concerns about college, namely the cost—and the cost of borrowing—are misplaced. We might wish tuitions were cheaper, but we're unlikely to see prices falling anytime soon (at least not without a huge government takeover of the industry, which, despite the rhetoric during the 2020 Democratic primary about making college free, seems unlikely). While it's not wrong to consider cost in the decision about if and where to go to college, focusing *solely* on cost can lead to decisions that don't serve us. None of us has the power to control what colleges charge for a degree. But we *can* control if and how we choose to pay for it. And only by being more aware and informed about the trade-offs can we make decisions that best serve our goals. In this book I'll explain how students and their families can go about managing the single most important, yet often overlooked, factor in how we pay for college: the *risk* involved.

2

Why College Sometimes Doesn't Pay

I f you are an aspiring student or the parent of an aspiring student, probably one thing about college keeps you up at night: the cost. The cost of college, with the debt that results from it, has become a national obsession. And reasonably so. Over the last two decades, prices in higher education have grown more quickly than prices in almost any other sector of the economy. That's how we got to the astronomical price tags that make headlines during every back-to-school season.

The high cost of college admission tends to raise the question, *Is a degree really worth it?* But once you recognize that the problem isn't really the price but rather the risk involved, you'll see that there's a more nuanced question you should be asking: not "Is college worth it?" but "When is college a good bet?" Thinking about it this way acknowledges the risk inherent in the transaction and invites a discussion of what choices or behaviors can make college pay, for you or your child.

When you hear the word *risk*, you might think of activities with a high degree of danger, like skydiving or motocross. But any circumstance that involves uncertainty, or some potential outcomes less favorable than others, involves risk. Going to college might not offer the same adrenaline rush as bungee jumping, but it's very clearly risky. The risk of primary concern to our discussion here is the risk of financial loss, either in absolute terms or relative to "what could have been." And with the cost of college at historic highs, the risk of pursuing a college degree that doesn't lead to the earnings you expected is, unfortunately, higher than ever.

Some college graduates win big, going on to high-paying professional careers or starting companies that generate a fortune. Those are the stories we like to celebrate to encourage young people to pursue education after high school. But in some cases, college actually leaves students worse off financially than when they started. Recognizing this risk will help you make decisions regarding college that suit your personal circumstances.

Uncovering the Risks

If I offered you the chance to invest $50,000 a year for four years and guaranteed you'd see a return of almost $1 million over the course of your career, you'd most likely take it without hesitation, right?

New research from Douglas Webber, a renowned education economist at Temple University, tells us that the typical college graduate will outearn the typical high school graduate without a college degree by $900,000 over the course of their lifetime. Even $30,000 in student debt, which is close to the average for new bachelor's degree recipients, seems like a small price to pay for such a bump.

It's these high average returns on higher education that have been compelling people to pay the ever-escalating cost of college for a generation now. But averages, as usual, don't tell the whole story. Here they might not even tell the most interesting part of the story.

What if I offered you the chance to invest $50,000 over four years, but instead of a guaranteed payoff, you'd have to spin a roulette wheel to determine your lifetime reward? The average reward across all potential outcomes is $1 million, but some pockets are worth more and some pockets are worth less. You needn't be a gambling aficionado to appreciate that the latter is a worse deal. In such a scenario, the price wouldn't be your primary concern. It's risk you have to worry about. Luckily, in the case of college (if not in Vegas) there are choices you can make to shift the odds in your favor.

It's helpful to think of the investment in higher education as being less akin to spinning a roulette wheel and more akin to investing in the stock market. Just because the stock market grows each year by an average of 7 percent doesn't mean that each individual stock grows by that amount. Nor does it mean that the entire market grows by that sum each year. The level of risk varies both across the individual investments you choose and across time. College has the same characteristics.

Webber's research highlights the fact that while the typical college graduate will outearn the *typical* high school graduate by nearly $1 million over the course of a lifetime, not all college graduates are "typical" in this way (just as not all investments yield the typical 7 percent return). Specifically, his analysis showed a swath of college graduates who not only had failed to see that nearly $1 million bump but had failed even to match the level of earnings of the typical worker with just a high school diploma. According to Webber's estimates, as many as 13 percent of college graduates would fall into this category: essentially a rough but conservative measure of who ends up worse off for having gone to college.

Of course, some of those people may have consciously chosen a path that didn't lead toward a financial return. They aren't necessarily victims of the college gamble. Imagine someone who opts to pursue a fulfilling but not financially rewarding career path, or someone who chooses to work part time or to accept a lower-earning occupation in order to devote more time and energy to parenting. As long as the choice is a conscious one, there's nothing inherently wrong with choosing a path that doesn't "pay." And to make conscious choices, every aspiring student should know the level of risk they are willing to tolerate and be fully informed about the risk associated with the range of possible outcomes. Unbeknownst to aspiring students, many known pitfalls can stand in the way of a generous or even adequate return on educational spending. Students who recognize these pitfalls and seek to avoid them can greatly improve their chances of reaping the anticipated benefits of education after high school. And while it's an unpopular view, appreciating these risks could appropriately discourage some students from enrolling in the first place.

To appreciate, and perhaps even mitigate, these risks, it can be helpful to understand that the sources of risk can be divided into two categories: systemic and idiosyncratic. Investing in a college degree introduces both types of risk. And within both categories, some risks—what economists would call endogenous risks—can be mitigated by your actions, and some—known as exogeneous risks—are fully or largely out of your control.

Systemic risk is the sort of risk that affects everyone equally, or at least somewhat equally. For instance, the risk of graduating in a recession is a systemic risk. It's also an exogeneous risk; there isn't much anyone can do to avoid that sort of bad luck. During an economic downturn, where one chooses to enroll or what one chooses to study could make a difference on the margin, but everyone is largely facing the same bad luck of having graduated at a time when fewer employers are hiring, and when those who are may be offering less generous compensation than they'd be offering otherwise.

Idiosyncratic risk is largely individual or circumstantial. The risk of sinking money into tuition and not graduating, for example, is largely idiosyncratic. While there may be occasions when events in the macroeconomy cause waves of people to drop out of college, more often it's individual circumstances they have little control over—like a health problem, a sick family member, challenges with childcare, or some other financial pressure—that cause people to give up on pursuing a degree. Other potential risks that fall under this category include taking too long to graduate, picking the wrong major, or unwittingly choosing a lemon college. These risks are largely endogenous; they often hinge on your individual choices. In this chapter, I'll highlight some common risks along the road to a degree that can leave students worse off than if they hadn't enrolled in the first place—and explain how to either mitigate or prepare for them.

Not Graduating

I'd venture a guess that if you are currently starting on the path toward a college degree, you are expecting to finish it. You'd likely be shocked to learn that just six out of every ten students who start a degree will ever finish. Even if you were aware of that fact, you might assume you'd be among those who beat the odds. You don't need to be a raging narcissist to fall into this common trap. We're all prone to overconfidence, a common cognitive bias—the tendency to overestimate one's own abilities with respect to one's actual performance or others' performance.

Theoretically, half of the credits needed for a college degree, earned at half the cost of a whole degree, would yield half the return of a degree in lifetime earnings (estimated at roughly half a million dollars). Unfortunately, for the majority of students who enroll but don't graduate, the reality isn't anything close to that.

There is very strong evidence showing that the access to higher earnings comes largely in a single lump when the degree or credential is completed, which means that getting halfway through a degree doesn't get you half the financial return you could expect if you had gotten your diploma. That's because the rewards of an investment in education kick in only after a student has entered the workforce with a new degree or credential: what is commonly referred to as the sheepskin effect. (The name originates from the fact that college diplomas were once printed, or written, on parchment made of sheepskin.)

This book was going to print in the fall of 2020, the "semester that wasn't" for many students. In order to combat the Covid-19 pandemic and prevent campus-based outbreaks, many colleges chose to move their services online, offering classes only or partly through virtual platforms—in most cases, with no reduction in price. Despite the radical degradation of quality and elimination of the social opportunities offered by an in-person experience, the vast majority of students remained enrolled as they had planned. There was no mass defection from college; in fact, there was barely any defection at all. That's because these students, who were most often stuck paying full freight, recognized that it was the *credential* they were really paying for. And even in the absence of all the myriad benefits of in-person education, it was worth it.

In theory, the labor market could reward workers for years of education credits completed rather than degrees achieved. Employers could consider the skills developed in coursework completed, rather than the credential. Then they could hire people with the skills that suited their needs and could pay them according to their value. A small number of employers do, but the data tells us that the majority don't.

The reason is twofold. First, that alternate method for finding and evaluating talent is expensive. Using an easily measurable indicator, like whether a potential worker holds a degree, and from where, streamlines the hiring process and saves money. The second reason is that correctly or not, many employers assume degree completion to signal something about a worker that employers value: for example, "So-and-so is the type of person who can finish things they begin, like their college degree, and that's the sort of person we need on our payroll." Though the former probably drives the sheepskin effect more than the latter, both likely play a role.

It's a phenomenon that makes investing in higher education riskier than most realize at the outset, because it means that if you don't graduate you're out not only what you spent or borrowed on your tuition and fees but also what you might otherwise have earned working for however long you are enrolled. It's like paying for Christmas gifts on layaway but getting neither the gifts nor your money back if you don't end up paying them off in full. In other words, going to college means putting a lot on the line.

So, why do so many people not graduate? Of course, the answer differs for each individual student, but a number of factors are typically at play in each instance of a student not finishing.

The most often cited reason for dropping out before graduation is financial constraints: students finding themselves unable to make ends meet and still afford the cost of enrollment. Too many students and their families forget that it's not just the cost of college they have to shoulder—it's the cost of college *plus* the cost of living. And today's students, who are likely to be older and supporting themselves and often their children, tend to have many more living expenses that could stand in the way of continuing their enrollment.

Sinking money and time into a college degree that you don't complete is among the biggest financial risks involved in attending college in the United States. But as we'll see in later chapters, it's also one that can often be mitigated or avoided.

Taking Too Long to Graduate

We often think of college as a four-year affair. In the movies, kids pack up the family car, move off to college, and emerge exactly four years later with the wisdom and practical skills needed to land a good job and become functioning adults. But that's not the reality for millions of today's students.

Even for students enrolled full-time, the path to graduation seldom takes the prescribed number of years. Though most bachelor's degree programs are intended to take four years, less than half of first-time students will graduate in four years or less, and 17 percent of bachelor's-degree-granting colleges in the federal student aid program graduate less than one-quarter of their students in four years.

Extended enrollment is very costly, perhaps more so than most students realize. Financing the extra cost of enrollment for a year at a four-year, private, nonprofit college will add almost $200 to your monthly loan bill for the next 20 years. Extending enrollment to six years would mean an additional $628 per month in loan payments.

But beyond the direct costs of extended enrollment, what many students fail to consider are the earnings they forgo while they remain in school full time: what economists call the opportunity cost. Taking an extra year to graduate takes a year's salary out of your lifetime earnings equivalent not to your salary upon graduating but to the salary you'll be making at the *end* of your career, unless a delayed graduation also leads to a delayed retirement. In either case, this opportunity cost will far exceed the direct cost of attendance for most people.

Moreover, almost 40 percent (7.7 million) of students enrolled in college in the United States today aren't enrolled full-time, often because they are juggling work, family, and other financial obligations. Unfortunately, among students who start their degrees enrolled part time, only 18 percent will earn any sort of credential within eight years. For those who don't graduate, part-time enrollment in college is the worst of both worlds: it's costly in terms of both time and money, and it never yields a return in the form of improved employment and earnings opportunities. And those who do graduate would have earned a higher return on their investment by enrolling full-time and entering the workforce sooner, even if they had to take on additional debt to do so.

The bottom line for both full-time and part-time students is that delaying graduation means delaying the opportunity to begin recouping their investment.

Choosing the Wrong School

When investors buy stocks or bonds in the financial marketplace, they make those decisions using extensive information on the historical return of these stocks. In fact, that's often the *only* piece of information people use when choosing investment vehicles, even though they represent an investment in a real living and breathing company. Similarly, when a gambler places a bet on a horse race, they generally do so by consulting win-loss records from past races. That's because statistically speaking, past performance happens to be a good predictor of future performance.

You might expect that investing in education would involve a similar calculus, but you'd be wrong. Investing in higher education is more akin to walking into a horse race and betting on a horse on the basis of the sheen of its coat or the color of its saddle pad.

If you have ever shopped for college, you are likely familiar with *Princeton Review*, which for decades has enjoyed a sterling reputation in the realm of college rankings. Many of us can recall flipping through their voluminous digests of American colleges as we contemplated where to apply. We all believed these rankings to be the best and only way to assess the quality of our options. Unfortunately, we probably didn't realize that the data was lacking an important feature.

These rankings (and others like them, such as *U.S. News & World Report*'s) are based largely on factors unrelated to student outcomes: cohort SAT scores, alumni giving, expenditures, reputation (assessed through a survey of administrators at competing institutions), and so on. While the current methodology employed by *U.S. News & World Report* for ranking schools does account for graduation rate, which is an important predictor of financial success, rankings generally fail to incorporate any information about earnings opportunities for students following graduation—though more than 90 percent of college goers report improved employment opportunities as a top motivation for enrolling in college.

While extensive information on how students fare after attending different colleges has long been available to regulators, they have only recently started to make it available to students through a little-known website, hosted by the US Department of Education, called the College Scorecard. Using this tool when shopping for college will allow you to find out how much previous graduates of each college are earning and how much they paid and borrowed to get through.

Similarly, *Money* magazine has only recently begun publishing a series called "The Best Colleges in America, Ranked by Value," which includes data like the level of average earnings for graduates. It also publishes rankings that weigh the up-front cost of enrollment against future earnings to award schools a rank based on the financial value, or return on investment, they provide.

PayScale.com is another new source that students can use to

understand the value in different options. Each year, they publish a list of almost two thousand colleges and the financial return on investment these have yielded for their former students over the course of twenty years. Here the differences across colleges become painfully apparent.

At the top of the list are prestigious schools like Harvey Mudd College and MIT, where the cost is high but the earnings of graduates are even higher—high enough to more than offset the seemingly exorbitant price tag. Despite their quarter-of-a-million-dollar all-in cost (for a four-year degree), each boasts a more than $1 million return on investment over the course of twenty years. But you'll see that lesser celebrated schools also rise to the top when evaluated on the basis of long-run value: for example, the Albany College of Pharmacy and Health Sciences and the Stevens Institute of Technology. And you'll notice that the low- (or no-) cost military academies, like US Merchant Marine Academy, US Military Academy, and US Naval Academy, are high on the list and offer a twenty-year return in excess of $1 million. Their graduates may not earn quite as much as graduates from Harvey Mudd or MIT, on average, but they have a smaller bill to pay before they start earning.

It wouldn't be unreasonable to assume that the schools ranked highly by publications like *U.S. News & World Report* and *Princeton Review* would be the same schools whose graduates go on to make the most money, but this is not always the case. For example, the Colorado School of Mines, a public engineering and applied sciences school in Golden, Colorado, ranks seventh in PayScale's value-based rankings, with an estimated average twenty-year return on investment of $1.03 million for in-state students (and just shy of $1 million for out-of-state students who face higher tuition), but it comes in at number 84 in the list of best national universities from *U.S. News & World Report*.

A quick click on the College Scorecard website can also reveal the *worst*-performing colleges on this measure. Places like Voor-hees College, Miles College, Maine College of Art, Talladega College, and Morris College sit at the bottom of the list, with an estimated average lifetime *loss* ranging between $190,000 and $160,000, suggesting that their students are worse off financially than people who never went to college.

Of course, it's important to point out that value-based estimates—like those from PayScale, the College Scorecard, and *Money* magazine—are not causal in nature. That means it would be wrong to interpret these numbers as the "effect" of having gone to a particular school. All colleges have inherent characteristics that may influence average earnings. For example, a college serving ambitious students may report better outcomes than one serving less ambitious students, even if the quality of their educational services is equivalent. And a college located in a region of the country with lower wages, on average, will likely report lower-earning graduates than an otherwise similar college located in a more affluent part of the country with higher average wages. This makes the data a bit trickier to interpret but certainly doesn't render it worthless.

What this data does illustrate is that from a purely financial standpoint there are clear winners and losers when it comes to picking a college that can deliver a financial return. Of course, future earnings are just one of many criteria to consider when making this important decision about where to enroll. But they are invaluable for mitigating the risk of wasting time, money, and effort on a degree that doesn't pay off in the job market.

Yet most students enrolling at low- (or negative-) value institutions probably aren't aware of what they are getting themselves into. Since parsing through data on individual campuses takes time, some might seek rules of thumb or tips they can use to rule out (or in) groups of colleges. For instance, are state colleges a safe bet? Do private colleges deliver better returns than public ones? Does geographical region matter? And so on.

Unfortunately, it turns out that there are no hard-and-fast rules. For example, you might imagine that acceptance into an Ivy League university would be akin to finding the golden ticket, at least when it comes to future earning opportunities. But new government data published in 2017 revealed that even some programs at elite universities were consistently leaving graduates without a pathway to economic security. One egregious example was Harvard's graduate theater program, whose alumni reportedly had average earnings of $36,000 a year and owed, on average, $78,000 in annual student loan debt. (For anyone scrambling to cross that one off your list, you can rest easy knowing that it has since shut its doors to new applicants, in large part because of this revelation, which was reported widely, and somewhat gleefully, by the popular media in what can only be described as a tremendous display of schadenfreude.)

On the other hand, an aspiring videogame designer might be surprised to learn that the top-rated program in this field can be found at the for-profit DigiPen Institute of Technology, which boasts a concentration of coursework in this and other tangential fields. Despite a pretty steep price tag, they boast a relatively high rate of graduation and good employment outcomes. Nearly half of students finish their courses on time, and graduates in their top field of study, computer programming, go on to have median annual earnings of $74,500. That's well above the national average and leaves students who finish their degree with a healthy return on investment and greater opportunity in a field where it's often challenging to get a foothold.

While students of my generation were making decisions about college using information from student surveys and marketing material from the colleges themselves, today's student has access to increasing amounts of hard data on where a particular program of study is likely to take them. So do your homework. If you're like most people, this will be among the biggest investments of your lifetime. And in the same way that you wouldn't invest in a car without kicking the tires and reading the reviews or a house without having it inspected and walking through it yourself, you shouldn't enroll in college without digging into the data on how previous students have fared in the labor market after graduation.

In chapter 3 I'll delve more deeply into exactly where and how to find that data, and how to use it to assess the options available to you. I'll help you identify your personal goals for college, financial and otherwise, and prescribe the best approach for choosing a school that will yield generous returns.

Picking the Wrong Major

When you're thinking about the return on investment for your degree, it's pretty well understood that your major is an important factor. I have the privilege of being able to travel the country to talk to all sorts of people about the economics of paying for college. At each talk, without fail, an audience member or fellow event participant will raise a question or comment about students failing to see a return on their degree because of having chosen a worthless major, like "basket weaving" which has somehow become the quintessential (and I assume deliberately comical) example of a worthless degree. At an event last year, one of the participants offered the example of "feminist basket weaving" (the sardonically applied modifier very clearly reflecting the political leanings of the audience).

Needless to say, we aren't facing a crisis of overenrollment in basket weaving (or feminist basket weaving) degree programs. But this bit of hyperbole does reflect the reality that some majors are much less likely to yield a high return. The absurdity of the example also seems to suggest that students who choose a worthless major should know better. After all, you'd basically need to live in a cave to think that a preposterous program of study like basket weaving would lead to an abundance of career opportunities.

This understanding explains why so many of today's students are choosing between majors like communications and engineering, or management and information technology, all of which are widely assumed to be a ticket to prosperity in the twenty-first-century economy. But what about all the majors that fall somewhere in between "safe bets," like computer science or business administration, and much riskier majors, like the well-worn (if preposterous) example of basket weaving?

It turns out that the financial return on one's higher education varies widely even across these "in-between" programs of study. An analysis by Douglas Webber, aforementioned professor of economics at Temple University, shows that the median lifetime earnings of the highest-earning major, chemical engineering, exceed the median lifetime earnings of the lowest-earning major, theology, by a factor of more than two and a half, meaning that the median chemical engineering major will earn 2.5 times more than the theology major over a lifetime.

It may not come as a shock to learn that in general, STEM (science, technology, engineering, and math) majors end up with the highest lifetime earnings, and humanities and arts majors end up with the lowest. But the relationship between major and earning power isn't always so obvious: for example, would you have guessed that a degree in neuroscience yields the same median earnings as the arts?

Since nothing is ever simple, however, it's also true that the return on your major depends on where you're enrolled. We often hear about investment banks and consulting firms hiring arts majors from elite colleges into career pathways that can lead to very high earnings: a fact often cited as the rationale for deliberately choosing a lower-earning major. But students should be wary of extrapolating too much about their own outcomes from these anecdotes.

It's also important to appreciate that the choice of major might not be driving all of the variations in earnings. For example, it may be that students of higher general aptitude select STEM majors with greater frequency, and that their aptitude is what leads to higher levels of earnings rather than the skills they obtained through higher education. Moreover, much of the financial opportunity afforded to graduates is determined by factors unrelated to major, like parental wealth, geography, innate intelligence, and social connections. But regardless of how endowed a student may be with these advantages, it's important to appreciate that becoming wealthy by majoring in theater or fine arts is a long shot.

Our discussions about this issue have often been focused on hyperbolic examples partly because, until very recently, we have lacked easy access to data about how financial opportunity varies by major. Even today, the information we have is relatively limited. But students still needn't and shouldn't choose a major blindly. The choice of where to go, what to spend, *and* what to study should be informed by data on student outcomes.

In chapter 4, I'll take a closer look at the role of majors and equip you with the resources and tools you'll need to pick a major with the best odds of paying off.

Bad Timing

Unfortunately, there are cases where a student makes all the right choices and simply gets dealt a bad hand. One source of systemic, exogenous risk—meaning risk that is not tied to your individual circumstances, or to decisions you can control—is the labor market. The returns on one's investment in college depend critically on what happens once one graduates. And those returns will generally take a dive for students unlucky enough to graduate into a depressed economy.

If you ask those who graduated from colleges, even elite ones, during the early 2000s they'd probably tell you that graduating during the collapse of the dot-com bubble has had a lasting negative impact on their earnings. And research would back them up. Till von Wachter, professor of economics at UCLA (and coincidentally a member of my dissertation committee many moons ago), has done extensive research on the cost of graduating from college during a recession. His work shows, with a high degree of precision, not only that graduating during a downturn leads to depressed wages upon graduation, but also that those wages don't bounce back even when the economy does.

Anyone who graduated from college in the spring of 2020 is likely already familiar with at least the first piece of this dynamic. Those students graduated into a job market that was severely and unexpectedly devastated by the economic fallout from the deadly Covid-19 pandemic. Over the course of just two months (two months smack dab in the middle of job-recruiting season) the economy lost twenty-two million jobs. The prospects for these students, who weeks prior had anticipated entering the workforce during a record-breaking economic expansion with record-low unemployment, plummeted.

The reality wasn't lost on these students, many of whom flocked to graduate school to prevent their poorly timed graduation from permanently marring their earnings prospects. Others took a more aggressive approach to their job search, some with the help of college administrators like David Greene, then the president of Colby College, who took it upon himself and his team to find high-paying jobs for each and every one of their five hundred graduates.

Unfortunately, an economic downturn isn't the only unanticipated market event that can degrade the value of a college degree. Suppose you've decided to take what has been sold as a sure path to solid employment and invest in a degree that prepares you to work as a radiologist. You graduate, land a stable and high-paying job, and celebrate having won the college gamble.

But soon enough you begin hearing things that make you nervous. You turn on the TV only to hear talking heads predicting the demise of your profession on CNBC. And then you open the latest issue of the *Journal of the American College of Radiology,* a respected trade journal, and learn that "the advent of computers that can accurately interpret diagnostic imaging studies will upend the practice of radiology." That's when you realize that technology and innovation are slowly but surely eroding the value of your education.

Sometimes the erosion of value can come in an instant. That's exactly what happened in the spring of 2019, when many graduates saw their livelihood upended by the sudden and unanticipated trade war with China under the leadership of President Trump. Virtually overnight, some people with degrees in agricultural production technology, agriculture business management, and agricultural biotechnology suddenly found that the trade restrictions had decimated the market value of their specific skill set.

Industries can be disrupted in any number of ways. And when people have invested in skills that are specific to a disrupted industry, they may find themselves with a credential that is not worth what it once was. This is just another way in which college is a risky venture.

Mitigating the Risks

The reason it's helpful to categorize the risk students face when investing in a college degree is that understanding the nature of the risk can help us to mitigate it. Here again we can borrow from financial economics to characterize the tools that exist to reduce students' exposure to risk.

Whereas some types of risk stem from external events or circumstances, other types arise when students and their families don't have access to the information needed to make an informed decision about where to go, what to study, and how to pay for it. In other words, a big reason that college sometimes doesn't pay is that we often make the leap into it with our eyes closed. Just as smart investors in the stock market don't make investments based on the charming appearance of the company's CEO on CNBC, or on a recommendation by their favorite pop-finance personality (okay, some probably do), you shouldn't choose where and how to go to college solely on the basis of a school's reputation or its listing in so-and-so's ranking of top colleges. Just as a savvy investor would study historical data on the returns of an equity they were considering, you too should examine the data that's available about how students at different colleges and in different majors have fared in the past. In taking a gamble on college, you're always going to know less than the colleges themselves about the quality of the service they provide, but minimizing that information asymmetry (i.e., the extent to which colleges know more than you) will go a long way in reducing the risk of the investment you're making in yourself. In chapters 3 and 4 I'll walk you through a method and the resources for evaluating the colleges you're considering.

Policy makers have a role to play here too. They could easily further promote the efforts to put data on employment outcomes by college and major into the hands of aspiring students. They could hold colleges to higher standards of transparency in order to gain access to federal student aid, which is and forever will be seen as an implicit endorsement from the government. They could also require disclosure of pricing information much as they do for financial investment by compelling colleges to deliver financial aid award letters on an accelerated time line and with a government-designed template that makes it easier for students to understand what their "aid" package actually includes. Reducing barriers to information is the low-hanging fruit when it comes to making college less risky for students.

Unfortunately, even once you've done all of your homework and know exactly what you're signing up for, there is still going to be uncertainty about what opportunities your college experience will provide. That uncertainty is risk. When information asymmetries *aren't* the driver of risk, we have to be a bit more creative with solutions. That's where strategies like hedging and diversification come into play.

Hedging is a strategy to mitigate risk by trading some of the potential upside in order to reduce the potential downside. This might seem like highfalutin strategy employed by stock traders managing complex investment portfolios, but it's one that many of us employ in day-to-day decision-making. For example, in her book *An Economist Walks into a Brothel,* financial economist Allison Schrager describes how a sports fan can hedge against the risk of soul-crushing disappointment in the event that their favorite team loses a big game by betting against their own team to win. If the team loses but the fan has at least won some cash, that should, in theory, offset a bit of the disappointment. But that also means that their elation in the event of a victory will be tempered by having lost money by betting against their team. When we hedge our bets, reducing the risk means being willing to also accept lower potential rewards.

In chapters 5 and 6 I'll explain how to use federal student loans and some innovative financial tools to reduce your financial risk further, in essence insuring your investment to ensure the payoff you're after.

Perhaps the most basic and well-understood strategy for mitigating risk in financial investing is diversification. Those of us fortunate enough to be able to save for retirement know that it's unwise to put all of our metaphorical eggs in one basket. Rather than investing our entire 401k in a single stock, we invest in a diversified portfolio: that is, one that puts those eggs in several, or even hundreds, of different stocks. By spreading our risk across a wide range of different investments we lessen the risk associated with any single stock.

In theory, this strategy could be employed when investing in college as well. The traditional model for a college degree, in which students invest a lot of money—and a number of years of their lives—in a single institution and a single course of study is akin to a highly undiversified portfolio. Students on this path are exposed to a tremendous amount of risk: if, for example, the school they're enrolled in closes, or loses standing or status in the eyes of employers, they will recoup far less of their investment than they might have otherwise. And because degrees are so expensive, they won't necessarily have the ability to start all over again.

This risk exists because our system bundles educational services together so that students have no choice other than to buy them as a package deal. However, there is a movement to change all of that. Many in the business community are rallying behind modes of education that deliver both skills and credentials in more of an "à la carte" manner. Examples include subdegree credentialing, which allow students to receive credentials—sometimes from multiple different institutions—indicating competencies in specific skills; boot-camp-style learning, in which students spend just a short period of time training on a specific and measurable set of skills; virtual education, which strips out the on-campus living aspects of the cost; and competency-based education (CBE), which requires students only to demonstrate competency to earn degrees and doesn't compel them to spend time in a classroom when it isn't necessary to learn a skill. All of these new models are in effect ways of unbundling the traditional college experience to allow for a more diversified approach to investing in higher education.

In chapter 7 I'll explain how some innovative approaches to higher education can help you gain the skills or credentials you need to get ahead in your career without necessarily going all in on an all-inclusive college degree.

College, as it turns out, isn't *always* a golden ticket to riches. Rather than looking at college as a guaranteed path to social or economic prosperity, we should all recognize it as a tool that enables us to invest in ourselves and our futures.

To increase your odds of that investment paying off, avoiding the pitfalls outlined in this chapter is a good place to start.

Picking a College That Pays

I bought my first home, with my husband, in 2017. Despite having professional expertise in policy, economics, and finance, I still could barely believe how many speed bumps exist in the process of buying a house: practices, policies, and procedures designed to ensure that the purchase is a wise one. We hired a real estate agent to lend expertise to our search and an inspector to give the house a thorough checkup once we had found one that we loved. Then the mortgage company put us through our paces to prove we could afford it. They wanted to ensure—rightfully so—that we were taking out a home loan we'd be able to repay. And then there was the pile of documents we signed on closing day to seal the deal—insurance forms, deeds, inspection certificates, and so on—many of which served to protect our investment, should it turn out that we had unwittingly purchased a lemon of a home.

The process was riddled with caution. The sellers were suspicious of our commitment and ability to buy. We were suspicious of the value and condition of the house. And the mortgage company was suspicious of our ability to repay our loan. The result was a complex process that included myriad signatures, confirmations, and due diligences. And while I can't say we particularly enjoyed it at the time, we recognized that the seriousness of the process matched the seriousness of the investment that we were making in our house and that the bank was making in us. For us, as for many or even most Americans, the purchase of that home will be one of the largest expenditures of our lifetimes.

For many, college tuition will also fall into this category. Yet the process by which most of us approach that investment is far less rigorous. Unlike the road to homeownership, which is paved with policy constraints and warnings of "buyer beware," the road to college is lined with cheerleaders telling aspiring students that a college degree will be a golden ticket to success. The result is student loans handed out with very little due diligence as to whether the student will be able to pay back—and how quickly—and students throwing buckets of cash at institutions that do precious little to safeguard their investment.

Colleges and universities, with the help of their powerful lobby, have succeeded in getting most Americans—and not just aspiring students—to believe that they are, largely, benevolent institutions. Most colleges and universities, despite their sometimes-massive revenues and stockpiles of cash, aren't on the hook with the IRS. Their designation as nonprofit entities exempts them from having to pay the federal taxes that would otherwise be due. Their position as institutions above scrutiny has even been formalized in the courts, where plaintiffs, like those suing for tuition refunds during the Covid-19 closures, will often be thwarted by a legal precedent called the argument of "academic deference," which discourages federal courts from meddling in matters of academia. Every facet of society seems to be sending the signal that colleges and universities are beyond reproach.

Though companies such as Google, Apple, and Facebook are

often grilled by the media and public officials about their use of our personal data, we apply nowhere near the same level of scrutiny to the institutions of higher education that stash mind-boggling sums of money in their endowments while still charging a price that exceeds the annual household income for more than half of American families. For example, the richest college in America, Harvard University, manages an endowment of nearly $40 billion and has a current all-in sticker price of nearly $70,000. That's a cash flow and balance sheet situation that we'd hardly let a company in any other industry get away with without ample suspicion and antagonism. But in our culture, Harvard, and other elite schools, are untouchable; they are held up as the gold standard.

I fear that our collective worship at the altars of higher education has led a generation or more of young people to enroll in college without realizing what, exactly, they are signing up for. That's not to say that colleges and universities are necessarily nefarious actors. But our lack of attention to the details of their practices and the financial transactions in which we're engaging has left the door open for nefarious or even neglectful behaviors. We've made a practice and a culture of giving colleges the benefit of the doubt. And the result is that people of all ages are making decisions about college blindly, despite the potentially grave financial consequences.

Many years ago, I partnered with a few colleges on an experiment to test whether we could improve students' notoriously low level of financial literacy, especially regarding their loans, by sending them informational material via mail and email. It was inspired by a program at Indiana University that claimed to have lowered their students' levels of debt by simply sending them letters about how much they had borrowed while they were enrolled.

In setting up the experiment, I had the opportunity to sit with many financial aid professionals. When I described the goal of our research—to help student borrowers acquire a deeper under-standing about the debt they were accumulating—at one of our initial meetings, one financial aid officer interrupted my rehearsed spiel about the project we were proposing to inform me that my goal was completely out of touch. She suggested that if I were to approach a random student on their campus as ask them how much they had borrowed, or even how much they were paying for school in the first place, they wouldn't have any idea. The nuance I was trying to impart on them, she explained, would be lost; they didn't even have a grasp on the basics.

As an economist and a generally persnickety consumer, I was astounded. How could so many young people be making such consequential decisions without this most basic of information about the financial trade-offs they were making? How could they determine whether they were receiving an education worthy of its price tag if they didn't even know how much their education was costing?

It turned out, as it always does, that the practitioners knew far more about their students than we did, the researchers with a lofty (some might say out-of-touch) plan to make things better. The ex-periment revealed that the information we delivered to students did absolutely nothing to improve their understanding of their debt levels and the consequences for their future budgets. But in the process we were able to confirm what the financial aid profes-sionals already knew to be true: for the most part, students were shockingly unaware of how much they were borrowing or paying for college, and some didn't even realize they were borrowing at all. Just over half the participants in our experiment (52 percent) were able to correctly identify (within a $5,000 range) what they paid for their first year of college. The remaining students under-estimated (25 percent), overestimated (17 percent), or said they didn't know (7 percent).

We later confirmed that this was not a phenomenon specific to the one college we had partnered with. When we replicated the exercise using nationally representative data, we found that about half of all first-year students in the United States seriously underestimate how much student debt they have and less than one-third provide an accurate estimate within a reasonable margin of error. And we found that among students with federal loans, 14 percent believed they didn't have any student debt at all. Imagine their surprise four years later when the first bill came in the mail.

In subsequent conversations with financial aid professionals, we got an inkling of why this might be the case. When we brought up the idea of sending student borrowers periodic financial statements informing them how much they were accruing in debt throughout their enrollment, some balked at even this most basic level of transparency. Much to my surprise, they expressed concern that reminding students how much they were paying or borrowing would make them want to drop out. I know that these people had the best interest of their students at heart. They weren't trying to dupe anyone. They simply believed, as we did, that the best way for these students to succeed financially was to finish their degree. And they felt that shielding those students from the unpleasantness of knowing how much it was costing them was necessary to make that happen.

What is clear from this and much subsequent research is that the implicit cost-benefit analysis we do automatically for each of the economic transactions we make every day—everything from the big decisions, like purchasing a home, to how much we spend on groceries—is too often absent from the process of shopping for college. This reality might help explain why so many students graduate from college each year feeling victimized by their debt rather than feeling grateful for the opportunities that it facilitated. And it may also help explain another common cause of disappointment among students: inadvertently enrolling in a lemon college—that is, one that doesn't deliver the financial return on your investment of time and money that you're expecting.

Despite this gloomy prognosis, there is actually good news on this front. For today's aspiring students seeking an economic return on their investment, making an informed, evidence-based decision is easier than ever before.

How to Pick a College

There is no single right way to pick a college. Each student will have a unique set of motivations, and each will face unique constraints in terms of what is possible or even desirable. Sorry to say, there isn't a magic formula. But there are strategies that can help you make informed and financially savvy choices.

Before you even begin to "shop" for college, it's important that you know what you're looking for. Just like grocery shopping without a list leads to me bringing home things like double-stuffed Oreos and whatever gadget catches my eye at the checkout, shopping for college before you have a firm grasp on your values and goals can lead to decisions you'll regret, but on a much more consequential scale.

In basic economic theory, we imagine that the way people make decisions can be described by something called a "utility function." The utility function is basically a map of your tastes. You can plug in any options you face, and it'll tell you which would be the most fulfilling. Neat idea, right? Turns out that people are a bit more complicated than this notion would imply, but the thought is a good one that I find helpful in guiding me through all sorts of decisions.

As you approach the point of making a decision about college, try to imagine what your utility function looks like. What are the factors that would contribute to your satisfaction with your decision about college? And what are those that would detract from it? Getting a handle on these factors *before* you begin shopping for college is probably the single most important aspect of the process.

While popular culture often characterizes the college search as something akin to the search for a soulmate—a quest for a spiritual connection and a "special" feeling—most students have real, non-negotiable constraints on where they are willing and able to go. These constraints are determined by one's individual values and life circumstances and therefore have to come into play before we get the economics involved. For example, geography is often (but not always) a non-negotiable. Many have a need to stay close to home (or, alternately, get as far away from home as possible), for any number of reasons. Others may be dead set on lifestyle factors like a warm climate or access to a major city, while others will consider only schools that offer a liberal arts curriculum. We could parse the trade-offs involved in these decisions, but if they are truly non-negotiable then we can simply assume that the cost of compromise is too hefty to consider.

So the first step in your shopping process is to make a list of non-negotiables (preferences that are more flexible, or "nice to have," can come into play later, once we've gone about the business of ruling out any lemons on the list of places you're considering). It's also fine to not have any and to keep your options open.

Next, you need to make a list of schools that satisfy your non-negotiable criteria. There are college consultants and paid services that can help you with this step. But there's also a free resource called the College Navigator that's easy to use and comprehensive. If you have the time to do your own homework, this is the place to start. The College Navigator tool can be found on the website for the National Center for Education Statistics. (That's a government website, so if you've found it through a search engine just confirm you've landed in the right place by checking that your URL ends with ".gov.")

The College Navigator allows you to pull lists of colleges that satisfy your geographic requirement and filter those results by the type of degree you're seeking. You can also limit results to public versus private institutions, if that is a concern. Once you enter the criteria for your search, the website will return a list of schools that satisfy them, along with links to a page offering more in-depth information about the school, including size, setting (urban or rural), accreditation, athletics, financial aid, and admissions. The College Navigator also allows you to save your favorites and export the list of schools you're considering to an Excel spreadsheet, in case you're the kind of person who likes that sort of thing (no judgment). Once you've narrowed down your list to just the schools that satisfy your non-negotiables, you can get back to the economics and start examining the factors that determine the financial risk of enrollment.

Graduation Rate

You might expect that your first step in assessing the potential value of your different options would be to check the price tag. But you'd be wrong. That'll actually be our last step, for reasons I'll explain shortly. Instead, you will want to begin with an often-overlooked statistic: graduation rate.

Throughout my career, when speaking with people—experts and nonexperts alike—about the economics of higher education, I've found that one statistic garners more surprise than any other. Here it is: less than two-thirds of students who begin a bachelor's degree will go on to finish it within *six* years. Those odds are dramatically lower than most people realize.

Moreover, not all colleges are created equal when it comes to getting students across the finish line. And if you're trying to make a decision about where to enroll based on the economics, having an idea about how likely you are to graduate can have a big impact on the potential return you can expect. As discussed in the previous chapter, the financial returns on a college degree are delivered after you've graduated. So sinking money into a degree that you are less likely to finish means you are less likely to get the payoff—in the form of higher wages and rate of employment—that can make it all "worth it."

Since we know that most students (56 percent) take longer than four years to graduate, it's useful to use a more generous time line and look at what percentage of students graduate within four and a half or five years. But even looking at the rate of students graduating within six years reveals that many colleges fail to deliver. At 13 percent of colleges, the six-year graduation rate is less than 25 percent. That means that less than one-quarter of the students at those schools will manage to graduate in six years' time. Put another way, the odds of a student at one of these schools graduating in six years or less are just one in four.

There's no threshold graduation rate that necessarily makes a school a lemon (though one could argue that a school with a six-year graduation rate of 25 percent would qualify). Your individual tolerance for risk and desire (or need) to see an economic return should dictate which rates of graduation—or nongraduation—are acceptable to you.

And remember that while the data on how previous students fared doesn't necessarily indicate how you will fare, you shouldn't make the mistake of believing that you will beat the odds. Thanks to the overconfidence bias, we're all prone to believing that we are above average. But if you understand anything about how averages work, you know that we can't all be right. So, for all intents and purposes, it's best to rule out the possibility that you'll beat the odds when you're trying to sniff out schools that might be lemons.

Future Earnings

The next step in ruling out lemon colleges is to turn our attention to earnings. But again, you have homework to do before you start shopping.

When researchers examine the financial return on college degrees, they have a different task than the one in front of you. Researchers are making generalizations about the returns on higher education generally, and even when examining a single college or program of study, they are comparing the likely employment outcomes and earnings profile of graduates compared to the average worker with just a high school diploma. Fortunately, you have the ability to be much more precise.

The first step is understanding what *your* specific alternatives are. The typical earning opportunities of a worker with a high school diploma may differ significantly from the opportunities that are in front of you, for better or for worse. For example, say you live in or are planning to relocate to Las Vegas, Nevada, where casino jobs are plentiful and offer generous compensation, even for workers without college credentials. In that case, you'd want to see that a college you're considering has a track record of placing graduates into jobs with higher wages than the one you'd consider in the casino industry. Otherwise you'd be better off (in a strictly financial sense) not going at all. Or does your family own a business that would offer you a lucrative career path (that you would want to pursue) without a degree? If so, that should be your point of comparison. Or maybe it goes the other way, and your only realistic options for work without a degree are jobs paying minimum wage, which is unfortunately the case in many areas of the country, where unemployment rates are high and economic prosperity is scarce. If so, that should be the bar that you'd expect a college to clear.

And remember to consider both the direct costs like tuition and fees and the "opportunity cost" of not working, or working less, while you're enrolled. The additional earnings you can expect with a degree should not just beat the earnings you'd be able to get without one; they should beat those earnings by enough to compensate for these costs.

The College Scorecard

In 2013, the White House announced that it had a plan to provide a rating system for US colleges that would help students make smarter choices about where to go and how much to pay. In addition, the administration hoped (pending necessary legislation from Congress) that in the future it would also be used by regulators at the Department of Education to determine a school's eligibility for aid programs. Like most policy proposals coming from the White House, it quickly ignited a flurry of roundtables, "convenings," and lobbying activity around Washington, D.C., where I was living and working at the time. College presidents were quick to fill op-ed pages with their eloquent objections to colleges' being measured and quantified in this way. Essentially, they argued that the value of services they provided was immeasurable—rating it would be akin to measuring the length of a rainbow or the beauty of a sunset, apparently. I argued in response that they were trying to pull the wool over our eyes.

I wasn't keen on the plan, but for a very different reason. I loved the idea of measuring the results colleges were producing and holding them accountable, and I liked even more that results would be published for all to see. But I didn't love the way the architects of the plan intended to go about it, which would have obfuscated the very information that aspiring students would need to do the sort of cost-benefit analyses that I prescribe in this book.

The plan as originally conceived was to give each college a grade (perhaps on a scale from A to F, or something similar) based on a combination of outcomes like graduation rate and earnings, as well as on noneconomic factors like the diversity of the student body. The problem was that these criteria imposed a set of values on students rather than empowering them with the data to make decisions based on what *they* cared about. After months of public debate, the White House's efforts took a different tack. In the face of pretty broad opposition and internal reconsideration of the issue, the effort pivoted slightly to the creation of what is now known as the College Scorecard.

The College Scorecard is a website, hosted by the US Department of Education, that provides detailed information about the financial outcomes of students from every accredited college in the country. Available data includes what percentage of students graduate, the average net price students pay (after taking into account grants and scholarships), and the range of salaries earned immediately after graduation. These are key elements needed to complete rough cost-benefit analysis prior to enrollment.

When the College Scorecard was first introduced in 2015, it published information for each college by taking averages across all majors and disciplines. But critics pointed out that since earnings information was not broken down by specific major or program of study, the data did little to help potential students make savvier choices about what to study and where. In 2019, the College Scorecard finally published, for the first time, the median earnings for graduates from each different major at every accredited institution in the country (a step that had been planned by the previous administration but could not yet be implemented because of constraints on data availability).

The Scorecard, which lives at www.collegescorecard.gov, is, at the time of writing and likely for years to come, the single most authoritative source of information on colleges for aspiring students who wish to avoid the common pitfall of choosing a college or major that, from a financial standpoint at least, doesn't pay off.

In the absence of a crystal ball, data on how other students fared after graduating from different colleges is probably the best resource for predicting how you'll do if you follow in their footsteps. But there are limitations in using this data to predict your future. First, while it can tell you how graduates of any given college or university have typically fared in the past, it doesn't tell you how someone *like you* will likely fare in the future. At best, it can tell you how someone who is similar to the typical graduate from that school is likely to fare.

For example, while NYU's performing arts department might have a track record of placing many of their graduates on Broadway stages, I am confident that if admitted I would *not* have the same result simply because I am decidedly less talented than the pool of graduates who are represented in the data (unfortunately, this is a difficult variable to account for, since it is impossible to quantitatively assess our innate talents relative to those of previous cohorts of students).

The other limitation of the information published by the scorecard is that while it gives an indication of the *typical* outcome, it doesn't give a good sense of the *range of outcomes*. While the median income of graduates from the economics department from SUNY Albany, my alma mater, is nearly $40,000, anyone who goes directly to start a PhD will find themselves earning as little as $20,000 from a teaching or research assistantship stipend, whereas someone who goes on to work at an investment bank may collect annual earnings upwards of $100,000.

Because of these shortcomings, the College Scorecard is most useful for ruling out those lemon colleges that *don't* consistently produce economic returns that meet your needs, rather than for picking among several attractive and relatively comparable options. Put another way, this data does a poor job of helping you to distinguish between different shades of "good" but does a great job in helping you weed out the bad. The goal isn't to predict your future but to eliminate colleges that don't have a track record of producing the type of results you are aiming for.

The Price Tag

When choosing the colleges you will apply to, you can largely ignore the price tag. Yes, you read that correctly. There are a number of reasons why, but the most important is the fact that the published price tag tells you very little about how much you'd actually pay.

We hear a lot about the "sticker prices" for colleges. Those are the ones listed on college websites and the ones generally cited by the media during the "back-to-school" news cycle. But there's another, much more salient number that generally flies below the radar: the net price, or the price that a student actually pays. With college tuition, much as with used cars, sticker prices are seldom, if ever, paid in full. Most students receive financial aid from their institution and grants from state and federal governments that put the actual cost of enrolling far below the sticker price.

Unfortunately, the only way to know what you'd actually pay to enroll at any given school is to apply. Colleges and universities are required by regulation to publish "net price calculators" on their websites to help aspiring students anticipate how much they'd pay to enroll, but these calculators are notoriously unreliable. The result is that shopping using the cost-benefit-analysis approach must wait until you've been accepted (likely at some expense, unless you are eligible to have the application fee waived) and you've received your financial aid award letter. Until then, you're left to estimate a personal price tag based on a combination of what others before you paid (also published on the College Scorecard) and your best guess as to what you'll be awarded in federal or state grant aid (based on your income and wealth), since those amounts, too, are often unknown until the financial aid award letters are delivered to accepted students.

The other reason to ignore the "sticker price" is to avoid the common mistake of believing that price is an indication of quality. This is something that we as consumers do, often unconsciously, for a variety of products ranging from craft beer to cars. And we're even more likely to fall into this trap when we have difficulty directly assessing the quality of a product ourselves. For example, because I know very little about makeup, I often assume that cosmetics with higher price tags work better. But according to makeup artists and beauty bloggers, I'm mistaken.

Unfortunately, colleges are aware that consumers think this way and, while they'd never admit it, may purposely be inflating their sticker price in order to exploit this weakness. Remember, a big price tag is fine as long as it delivers a big payoff later on.

Publics and Privates and For-Profits, Oh My!

As your search for a college narrows, you may find that your list contains public colleges, private (nonprofit) colleges, and maybe even some for-profit colleges. For the most part, you can feel free to ignore these distinctions. While the term *private college* may connote higher prestige or pedigree, whether a college is designated as public or private is determined simply by its funding model. Colleges that collect revenue directly from state appropriations of resident tax dollars, and not just through the collection of state-funded scholarships, are considered public institutions. As you'd imagine, having some of the costs covered directly by tax dollars, before tuition-paying students even come into the equation, often means lower cost for students. And while this is not always the case, the amenities offered at public colleges tend to be more modest than the ones offered at private colleges, which also contributes to their lower total cost.

Despite that, public colleges—especially state flagship campuses like Ohio State University or the University of Michigan—often employ world-class faculty and deliver high-quality education. Unfortunately, the public-versus-private distinction doesn't tell you much about the educational experience or the economics of enrollment. Instead you'd be best off sticking with the sort of cost-benefit consideration we have been discussing and reviewing each college on its individual merits: the price you're likely to pay and the benefits you're likely to derive.

The distinction between for-profit and nonprofit private colleges is a bit more problematic. Historically, private colleges were generally designated nonprofit institutions. That meant they were exempted from paying taxes on the grounds that they were providing a public benefit. But over the past two decades we have seen a rapid increase in the number of private colleges operating with a for-profit tax status. You've likely seen advertisements on television and online for some of the bigger ones, like University of Phoenix and Strayer University. Because for-profit colleges have the explicit mission of enhancing the wealth of shareholders (like any other for-profit company), they are not afforded tax-exempt status.

As the number of for-profit colleges has risen, so has their share of the college market. Between the years of 2000 to 2010, enrollment in four-year programs at for-profit colleges increased seven-fold, whereas enrollment at the next fastest growing category of college (public nonflagship colleges) grew by just 41 percent.

Many observers of this growth were vocally skeptical that colleges with shareholders could offer students a college experience that was worth the price tag, which often exceeded that of public and nonprofit institutions by a very wide margin. In 2015, policy makers responded to this skepticism by announcing that colleges operating as for-profit companies would be subject to a new set of regulations, called Gainful Employment, which required them to show that their students were "gainfully employed" after graduation and could succeed in paying back their debt. The schools that fell short would get kicked out of the federal student aid program, which by and large a college unable to compete against other federally funded schools would effectively put them out of business.

The data released on the back of the new rules provided definitive proof that for-profit colleges were, more often than not, falling short of delivering financial returns for their students. As Mark Zuckerman, former Obama White House staffer, policy expert, and now president of the Century Foundation, wrote in a letter to the editor of *The Wall Street Journal,* "The worst for-profit colleges rake in millions of dollars in federally subsidized loans from low-income students, while too often leaving students owing mountains of debt and facing a lifetime of low earnings. Moreover, for-profit schools account for nearly 99% of all student fraud claims nationwide and spend significantly less of their tuition revenue on student instruction than public and nonprofit colleges." And according to a report by two top-notch economic researchers that was initially published by the Brookings Institution, 47 percent of students who graduated from for-profit colleges defaulted within five years, compared to 28 percent of all students who started paying back their loans in the same year. Given that these colleges tended to specialize in serving students who were more economically disadvantaged, these results were unacceptable.

Until that time, observers of education with a promarket outlook on the industry (me included) had argued that the tax status of a college doesn't determine its ability to provide a valuable service. That's still true in theory, but for the early crop of for-profit colleges it wasn't true in practice, so it's an argument that now falls on deaf ears. Those institutions peed in the pool, and now many observers want everyone else out of the water.

Interestingly, however, the regulation that was intended to rein in the for-profit colleges had an unanticipated side effect—putting some highly celebrated private, nonprofit colleges on the chopping block. Because some explicitly career-oriented programs of study at nonprofit colleges also fell under the purview of the higher standards set by the Gainful Employment Regulations, the release of data on student outcomes outed a few programs at very elite colleges for being just as "predatory" as the for-profit ones that had been so readily villainized by the public. For instance, the two-year drama program at Harvard University, which carried a price tag of $63,000, was churning out batch after batch of graduates who were quickly finding themselves with more debt and with insufficient earnings to justify the amount they had borrowed to pay for tuition. With the median student debt at $78,016 and the median annual earnings at roughly $36,000, program graduates were understandably making little progress in paying down their student loans. When that data was made public, pundits reveled in the opportunity to chastise the most celebrated and envied college in the country. But Harvard quickly shut down that party by announcing that it would suspend admission to the program.

Majors Matter

I wasn't much of a student in high school. I was much more concerned with having cool clothes and figuring out how to get boys to like me than I was with grades. (In retrospect, I would have been better off focusing my energy elsewhere, since I largely failed on both of those fronts.) So, when it came time to apply to college, I wasn't prepared to make a decision about what to study or where to go. But I did what I thought I was supposed to do and reluctantly began filling out applications.

During my senior year I went through the quintessential privileged-kid college search. My parents generously schlepped my irritable teenage self around the state to visit a variety of schools, some we'd never have been able to afford, some I didn't have a chance of getting into, and a few that were actually realistic options.

As much as I'd like to tell you that my decisions about where to apply, where to enroll, and what to study were based on sound economic reasoning, the truth is that my method was more akin to my two-year-old's when picking out his clothes in the morning. My passions were fickle, my process was haphazard, and I had no sense of what I was really trying to accomplish.

One thing I did know was that I was an artsy kid; I loved being involved with school plays and took art classes. So, in the spirit of "following my passion"—an adage I'd heard time and again—I halfheartedly prepared to begin a college career focused on "something artsy." (Yes, my ambitions were approximately that specific.) I prepared a portfolio for art school applications, filling it with all the doodles, paintings, and moody black-and-white photographs I'd produced during my high school years. I even worked with a voice teacher, briefly, to prepare a song for college auditions.

It was all quite romantic, the idea of moving away from home to immerse myself in the world of theater and the arts. But a part of me knew this wasn't a solid plan. While my family had enough money that I'd never really wanted for anything growing up (other than cooler clothes), I knew that once college was over I would be expected to start providing for myself. I had the sense that college was somehow supposed to connect me with that future.

One of the more poignant moments in my college search happened at Syracuse University, a school that was honestly outside of our budget but that my parents generously entertained anyway. My mom and I were meeting with an admissions officer from their design program to talk about my application. At one point, the conversation shifted away from the joy of creating art in their beautiful, well-lit studios to what types of job opportunities I could expect as an arts major after graduation. (I don't remember how it got there, but I'd be willing to wager good money that it was my mother's doing. While she and my father were supportive of the whole notion of following your passion, I know they were also concerned about my financial future.)

I remember the admissions officer informing me (a reality check I'm sure she'd given hundreds of times) that many of their fine arts graduates went on to a career designing everyday consumer products, like toasters and coffee makers, which was not particularly inspiring to me. Others, she added, got jobs designing wrapping paper, textiles, and illustrated greeting cards. Not exactly the image of an "artist" I had in mind, but I was still hanging in there. Then the admissions officer turned to me and asked: "Do you love creating art so much that you'd be willing to be poor for the rest of your life in order to pursue it as a career?"

Oof. I don't recall how I answered the question. It didn't really matter, because in that moment the fantasy had already begun to melt away.

You'd think that this conversation would have devastated me. But in reality, I felt grateful for that dose of pragmatism. Perhaps I appreciated it because it resonated with my yet-to-be-realized affinity for an economic way of thinking. While I was an artsy kid, I was also a very methodical one. I liked things to have order and reason. Heck, one of my favorite "toys" from childhood was a pink clipboard I'd gotten on a family road trip to Niagara Falls. For years, I used it to plan things like packing lists for trips and rules for different clubs I created with my friends. (I know what you're thinking; yes, I am still this much fun.)

The idea of "following my passion" was a nice one. And it was the only one I really recall being given as a framework for thinking about what to study in college. But at the same time, it didn't sit well with the pink-clipboard part of me that knew this decision needed more practical consideration than my passion could provide.

I ended up at Ithaca College, a small liberal arts school in upstate New York. I chose it for a few reasons. First, it was the "right" distance from home. I could have the sense of freedom that came from moving away but still be able to drive back for a weekend visit when I missed home. Second, it had a world-class musical theater program. I wasn't nearly talented enough to be any part of it and didn't harbor any delusions that I was, but I had a sense that its mere proximity would offer some intangible benefit.

I spent my first year racking up knowledge from all different classes, ranging from ballet to Economics 101. I also spent that year racking up a lot of student debt. My parents had generously offered to contribute to the cost of my education in an amount equal to what it would have cost to attend one of our in-state public colleges. But the private college I had chosen cost much more than that, and I had taken on loans to cover the rest.

Despite the summer camp–like experience I had arranged for myself, something didn't feel right. I was painfully homesick and felt uneasy about spending so much on an education that didn't seem to be leading in any clear direction. Soon I had to ask myself if the fun I was having was truly worth the money my family was spending, the debt I was taking on, and, perhaps more important, the future I was setting myself up for. I wasn't sure. But I knew one thing: I didn't really have the luxury of accepting this uncertainty. The clock was ticking, and in a few years I'd be expected to start paying my own bills.

That year I had another pivotal experience, one that might seem unfathomable to those of you who have sat through an introductory lecture on the principle of supply and demand: I fell in love with economics. Not only did I feel an immense satisfaction from the way economic models could take the most intractable problems and provide a framework with which to analyze them, but economics gave me a way forward, in more ways than one. It gave me the clarity and confidence to see that I wanted to be an economics professor—and a new way of thinking about the trade-offs implicit in that path. Looking at things through the lens of economics helped me see that the tuition and time I was investing in my education in Ithaca weren't in sync with my future plans.

At the end of the first year, I packed my entire dorm room into my silver Dodge Neon and drove home, knowing that I wouldn't be back the following fall. I didn't bother to tell any of my friends for fear they'd make a case for staying that would be too hard to ignore. But I knew that the value I would get out of three more years at Ithaca—with its relatively small economics department— wasn't going to justify the costs.

That fall, I enrolled in the economics department at the state university closest to my childhood home, SUNY Albany. When I walked into my first meeting with my assigned faculty adviser, I told her that I was going to be an economics professor. She knew full well that I hadn't a clue what I was signing myself up for, but she offered keen and generous guidance nonetheless. I still took art classes and sang in the university choir, but my long-term goal had come into focus, and with it the clarity to make an informed decision about where to go, what to study, and how to pay for it.

"Undecided"

In going away to college without a clue about what I was going to study, I was, in the jargon of college applications and admissions offices, "undecided." When you think about it, it shouldn't be shocking that as many as 50 percent of students enrolling in college do so without having declared a major or that 75 percent of students will change their major at least once before graduation; many young people aren't prepared to make a decision about what they want to do with the rest of their lives at the time they leave high school. And many expect that taking as many different kinds of courses as possible, for as long as possible, is the best way to decide.

That's a reasonable assumption, and pretty similar to the one I made myself. But it's also a potentially expensive one.

College is always a risky venture. We are all essentially playing the odds that our degree will ultimately yield access to opportunities that we value more than what we pay to attend. Going off to college without a clear path in mind means that you're making that bet with less precision than you could otherwise have.

Moreover, enrolling before you're really ready to pick a path may mean taking longer than necessary to graduate: it can add on semesters or even years of enrollment. For me, the cost of being undecided was basically the price of my first year at Ithaca. Almost none of my credits transferred. Without having made that stop, I likely would have graduated in three years instead of four.

At the time, I didn't fully appreciate the fact that there was another option for people like me who aren't sure what they want to study: the gap year. For young people especially, college doesn't need to be a "now or never" deal. In retrospect, I think I would have benefited from waiting a year to enroll. We associate the gap year with adventurous activities like building houses in Haiti or backpacking across Europe, but in my case, simply keeping my full-time summer job as a cashier at Home Depot would have bought me the time to do the soul searching necessary to make a more thoughtful decision about my future.

This too, however, is a trade-off. Delaying the start of college can mean delaying your entrance into the workforce, which means losing out on a year's worth of increased earnings. But for the undecided, *not* delaying can also have a cost. So, from an economic perspective, there isn't an obvious answer when it comes to taking a year off or not. It will depend on your individual circumstances and will be different for everyone.

The Myth of the "Good School"

As discussed in the last chapter, a cost-benefit analysis can help you to decide if and where to enroll and how much to spend. Some might assume that just going to a "good school" exempts them from having to do any further calculus. After all, isn't a degree from a "good school" enough to land you a job that will pay the bills? Unfortunately, no. In fact, from an economic perspective, where you go actually matters *less* than what you choose to study. And looking only at average earnings for graduates of a particular institution can be misleading, because it ignores the fact that earnings also vary significantly across majors.

For example, data from PayScale suggests that graduates from Harvard University have median earnings of $74,800 in the first five years following graduation. (Not surprisingly, Harvard graduates beat the median earnings for graduates across all four-year colleges by more than $20,000 per year.) But that striking sum obscures some important information about how graduates with different majors fare. Certain majors at Harvard, just like at other schools, yield far more earning power than others. For example, the median annual earnings for computer science majors one year after graduation is $128,900, compared to just $48,000 for history majors, despite these degrees having the same (or very similar) price tags. Not only is that a difference of more than $80,000 per year, but for many graduates it's also the difference between affordable versus unaffordable student debt. It might even be the difference between being able to comfortably buy a house, have children, or start saving for retirement relatively soon after graduation versus much later.

This phenomenon doesn't exist exclusively at places like Harvard. Take, for example, the University of Central Florida (UCF), which is among the very largest colleges in the country, with almost sixty thousand undergraduate students. The annual cost of attending UCF, including tuition, fees, and textbooks, is $7,568. Over four years, that amounts to a total cost of $30,272. But since the average bachelor's degree takes 5.1 years to complete, let's assume five years for a total cost of $37,840, not including the cost of living.

Now remember, the real cost of college isn't just the money you pay to be there: it also includes the opportunity cost of not working, or, in other words, what you'd otherwise be earning if you had a job. According to government surveys, the median worker without a college degree and in the beginning of their career (aged twenty-two to twenty-four) earns approximately $23,000 annually. So being in school for five years means you're giving up about $115,000 in income (you can adjust this amount by what you'd expect to earn working during summer or holiday breaks or if you'd have a lucrative opportunity available to you). When you add that opportunity cost to the direct cost of enrollment, you arrive at the all-in price of a degree from UCF: about $152,840.

Now let's suppose that you head off to UCF and don't have any idea what you'd like to study. The way you'd try to predict whether a degree from UCF will "pay off," in a strictly financial sense, would be to compare the overall median salary earned by graduates with what you'd be likely to earn if you entered the workforce with just a high school diploma. Let's do the math for that one (though once you understand the process it's easy to make other comparisons: for instance, you could compare a two- versus a four-year degree, or degrees from different colleges).

According to data from PayScale, the median annual earnings for early-career UCF graduates is $40,000. That beats the median annual earnings of early-career workers with just a high school diploma by a pretty wide margin—$17,000, to be exact. That's a good sign, but it's not the only thing to consider. Remember that in the long run the financial benefits of a degree continue to accrue over the course of your career. So let's say that you're expecting to work until you're sixty (the average age of retirement in the United States). And to make the math simple, let's say you're going to be twenty-five when you finish your degree. That means you'll have thirty-five years to put that credential to work earning a premium wage. Over that stretch, the median UCF grad will earn an extra $595,000 compared to the median worker with just a high school diploma. If you subtract the price of the degree that we just calculated—$152,840—the difference of $442,160 is an estimate of your potential return on investment. Sounds like quite a deal!

Median Earnings UCF Grad – Median Earnings H.S. Diploma = Annual UCF Earnings Premium
$$\$40,000 - \$23,000 = \$17,000$$

Annual Earnings Premium x Years Working = Lifetime $$ Benefit of UCF Degree
$$\$17,000 \times 35 = \$595,000$$

Benefit of UCF Degree – Cost of UCF Degree = Return on UCF Degree
$$\$595,000 - \$152,840 = \underline{\$442,160}$$

You should think of this approach less as a prediction and more as a rough estimate—a back-of-the-envelope calculation. It makes assumptions about things like age of retirement and the net cost of enrollment (after grants and scholarships), which can be easily adjusted for different scenarios. For example, if you were to retire at age sixty-five instead of sixty you would multiply your annual lifetime earnings by 40 instead of 35. But it also ignores more complicated factors like taxes; the general tendency of the college wage premium to grow with time; the fact that money earned at different points in life has different relative values (money today is always better than money tomorrow); and inflation. These too can be accounted for in your analysis, depending on how precise you wish to be. But for the purposes of getting an idea about whether the path you're on will pay off, it's a reasonable approach.

The bigger concern, however, is that this method examines median outcomes across *all* UCF graduates, while in reality outcomes can vary significantly, for better or for worse, across majors.

Once we update our cost-benefit analysis using the numbers specific to a given major, we paint a much more nuanced picture. For example, let's imagine that you're a fine-arts major. Whereas the median UCF graduate earns an additional $17,000 a year compared to workers without a college degree, UCF graduates with a degree in fine arts actually earn barely more, on average, than workers with just a high school diploma. According to the College Scorecard, graduates from their bachelor's program in fine and studio arts had median annual earnings of just $24,700. Without a sizeable premium in the earned wages, the odds are that an investment in a fine arts degree from UCF won't pay off—at least not in the strictly financial sense.

Now, degrees in arts are an easy target. Most people pursue them not to get rich, but for the enriching opportunities and intangible benefits they provide (the satisfaction of working in a creative field that you love, for example). And that's perfectly fine—as long as you're aware of the trade-offs you're making and can tolerate that level of risk. You could also make the argument that loving your profession probably means you'll work harder and be more successful. These are the kinds of things to consider once you've run the numbers and know what options you're working with.

The point is, you probably don't need math to tell you that an arts degree is unlikely to pay off financially. But you'd be surprised to learn how many majors that seem as if they *would* set you on a lucrative track in fact do not. For example, I'd imagine that most students majoring in communications and media studies at UCF believe it will lead to higher wages and improved employment opportunities. But the data doesn't really support this notion, at least not for the typical (i.e., median) graduate. Communications and media studies majors outearn workers with only a high school diploma by a relatively small margin, with median annual earnings of $27,800 in the first year out of school compared to the $23,000 we estimated for a typical worker with a high school diploma.

This pattern isn't unique to UCF: many schools have a few majors (or more) that don't yield a significant financial return compared to entering the workforce after high school. Of course, plenty of majors at UCF and elsewhere *do* yield an economic payoff; the point is simply to seek out this data so you can make a more informed decision, not only about where to enroll, but also about what to study when you get there.

My hope is that you'll take away from this exercise in basic arithmetic the realization that the "calculus" of college-going isn't beyond your grasp. With the principles just discussed, paired with your knowledge of your own personal circumstances, it's entirely reasonable for you to repeat this exercise to inform your own choices. Here's where to find the raw data that you'd use in an analysis.

Your number one stop should be the College Scorecard, which publishes median earnings, by major, for graduates one year after graduation for each school in the country. It also hosts information about the net costs former students have paid, broken down by family income. Until you've received information about your personal financial aid package, this could help you gauge expected costs (though these figures do include living expenses, so you might want to make that adjustment).

Another important resource is payscale.com, which publishes more detailed information on earnings, including an estimated twenty-year return on investment, an estimated annual return on investment, early and midcareer median earnings, and average earnings by major. Both data sources have their shortcomings, so

I'd recommend running the numbers in each and every way you can until you feel you have a grasp on the trade-offs in front of you.

How to Pick a Major

The best way to pick a major, like the best way to pick a school, is to first understand your goals for enrollment as well as your tolerance for risk. According to surveys, the vast majority of students who enroll in college are doing so to increase their earning potential or otherwise advance in their career. But because we are human beings and not just money-grubbing robots, we tend to have other objectives as well. Most students would understandably prefer to major in a subject that interests them, and one for which they have an aptitude or ability. Those things are tougher to quantify, but they are often just as important.

Your tolerance for risk has less to do with personal preferences and more to do with your specific financial situation. I knew that when I finished college I wanted to be able to support myself financially. So, when I decided to become an economics major, part of the appeal was the certainty it gave me that I'd be able to land a job that paid the bills right away. While I *might* have been able to pay the bills had I graduated with an "artsy" major, I wasn't willing to take the risk. If I'd had more of a financial safety net available to me at that time (and less innate distaste for uncertainty), I might have been more inclined to chance it. The risk involved in choosing a less lucrative major will be unique for each person.

If you have already narrowed down your list of schools, the most reliable resource for information on postgraduation earnings for various majors is the College Scorecard, as we just discussed. But if you're starting to think about what you might want to study and don't have specific schools in mind just yet, a recent report from the Georgetown University Center on Education and the Workforce offers a great place to start. In addition to ranking median earnings by major across all US colleges and universities, it offers an advantage over other similar analyses because it provides the 25th and 75th percentile of earnings, which will give you a sense of how widely earnings vary for each major. The figure below provides a nice overview across major categories.

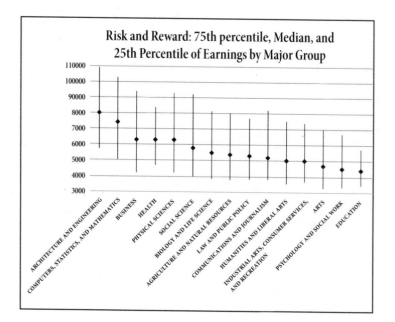

The general trends depicted above might not surprise you. As one would expect, STEM (science, technology, engineering, and math) majors all end up at the top of the pack, with architecture and engineering majors earning an impressive median income of $80,000—well above the median earnings for all bachelor's degree holders: $59,000. At the other end of the spectrum, too, there are few surprises, with arts, social work, and education offering median annual earnings of $47,000, $45,000, and $44,000, respectively. But just like looking at returns across institutions on the whole, looking only at these broad categories can obscure important variations across the specific majors they represent.

The detailed breakdown by specific major (found in the Appendix) is where things start to get interesting. For example, it reveals that while all types of engineers tend to do quite well, none can hold a candle to petroleum engineering majors, with their median annual income of $129,000: more than double the typical earnings for a bachelor's degree holder. And in the health category, we see that pharmacy and pharmaceutical sciences and administration majors seem to outearn all their peers, with median annual earnings of $110,000, compared to the $63,000 average across all health majors.

Unfortunately, not all the surprises found in this data are pleasant ones. For example, biology and health sciences majors aren't all created equal when it comes to making a living. The typical (i.e., median) graduate in this field will have an income of $55,000, but neuroscientists (despite their reputation for brilliance if not social skills) earn even less: just $47,000 annually. And despite the conventional wisdom that a career in business is always a pretty solid bet, a degree in hospitality management ($51,000) will set you up to earn far less than the typical business major ($63,000).

By looking at the spread between the 25th and 75th percentiles, you can also get a sense both of how much *more* you could potentially earn and how much *less* you're at risk of making, relative to the typical salary for that major. It would seem logical to assume that the riskiest majors are the ones that we think of as long shots, like performing arts, which tend to offer two potential outcomes: hitting it big or perpetually waiting for your break. But statistically speaking, the riskiest majors are ones that produce the widest range of outcomes: a group that includes some fields that we tend to think of as a reliable pathway to a well-paying career, like physics and economics. For example, the median income for economics majors overall is $73,000, but for the 25th percentile that sum is just $46,000—meaning that 25 percent of economics majors earn less than that amount. And on the flip side, the 75th percentile is $69,000, which means that earnings for only 25 percent of economics majors exceed that level. (In retrospect, my faith in economics as a pathway to a more certain financial future might have been ill-conceived.)

Degrees in physics seem to possess the same dynamic. While majors in physics, which is among the celebrated STEM fields, do just fine on average ($77,000), it turns out that there are both big winners and big losers, with 25 percent of physics majors earning less than $43,000, which is on par with (and actually a bit worse than) the median earnings of drama and theater arts majors ($44,000). On the flip side, 25 percent of physics majors end up earning more than $113,000 per year.

These variations in earnings aren't a fluke. Nor are they influenced by confounding factors, like some people having graduate degrees and others not; this data is based only on people with *just* bachelor's degrees.

In the Appendix of this book you'll find a summary table of this data, which has not previously been published in full elsewhere (to my knowledge), and which was generously provided for publication by the researchers at the Georgetown University Center on Education and the Workforce, who are renowned for their work in this area.

There's no right or wrong answer when it comes to deciding what to study. But informed and data-driven decisions will increase the odds of making the choice that's right for you.

Loans: The Smart Way to Pay

I f college is on the horizon for you or someone you love, the thought of borrowing to pay the tuition bills likely raises your heart rate a few ticks. After all, you have surely heard the horror stories about the proverbial distressed borrower, about to turn thirty and still living in his or her parents' basement. (Why do they always live in the basement? If my son ever moves home after college, I vow to let him live in his old bedroom on the main floor of the house. But I digress.)

Take a deep breath, because the reality is that student debt is far less risky than you probably imagine, as long as you've made thoughtful and evidence-based decisions about the education that debt is financing. In fact, even if you aren't expecting to have to rely on student loans to pay your tuition, you should read on, because I'm going to make the case that even when you have plentiful cash on hand, using student loans is (with a few caveats) the smart way to pay for college.

Part of what has made college riskier today than decades ago is that leveraging one's future welfare to make it happen has become the norm. In a sense, it's like taking a credit card to the casino to gamble money you don't have. While higher education pays big dividends on average, we also know that events outside your control—like recessions, policy changes, or innovation in your field—can erode the value of a degree, making loans more difficult to repay.

Sounds scary, right? Yes, it does. But fortunately for you, and for the millions of students who take on student debt each year, the things you likely don't know about student loans are pretty much all good news.

Student Debt: Not as Scary as It Seems

In 2014, researchers from an analytical consulting firm investigated the popular narrative about student debt by looking at the one hundred most recent news stories they could find about borrowers struggling to pay back their loans and compared the amount of debt each borrower had outstanding to the national average. What they found was that the average borrower featured in these stories had debt exceeding $85,000, triple the amount held by typical student loan borrowers. The anecdotes cited in the media coverage, it seemed, were generally extreme and nonrepresentative cases, hand-picked by reporters for being remarkable rather than typical. This isn't really too surprising. After all, the headline "College Graduate Pays Off Student Debt Through Affordable Monthly Loan Payments" probably won't attract a whole lot of eyeballs. The problem is that the constant stream of news stories focusing on borrowers in severe circumstances may be instilling an irrational fear of borrowing to pay for college—maybe even a fear that discourages aspiring students from enrolling in the first place.

In 2011, the often pessimistic but always thoughtful longtime analyst of higher education policy Kevin Carey wrote a compelling editorial for the magazine *The New Republic* challenging the narrative of destitute college graduates, who, upon finding their degree worth little more than the paper it's printed on, end up working as baristas or bartenders to make their monthly loan payments. When he reached out to people profiled in such stories to find out how they were doing decades later, he found that most had actually gone on to have illustrious careers. One ran her own human resources firm; another had risen to senior manager at an international consulting company; and another had gone on to earn a PhD and had landed a cushy gig as an analyst at a Washington, D.C., think tank. This, Carey notes, is "how things usually work out for those who get degrees."

The evidence isn't just anecdotal; if we look at the data, we see that most student borrowers take on an amount of debt that's reasonable for the return they can expect on their investment. For example, the typical graduate from a four-year college will have less than $30,000 in debt at the time they graduate ($28,500 to be exact): an amount that can be repaid with payments of less than $200 per month, or about 4 percent of the average gross monthly income for college-educated millennials. Moreover, borrowers who are truly facing hardship will in most cases be eligible to have their loans forgiven or monthly payments reduced.

This is not to say that student loans are completely harmless, or that cases of college-educated baristas struggling to make their ballooning loan payments don't exist. Plenty of people have made decisions about student loans they've later come to regret. But these instances are fewer and farther between than we tend to believe. To avoid that fate, it's important to gain a basic understanding of how student loans work. So in this chapter we'll look at the pros and cons of each of the various financing options available to you so that you'll be well equipped to make responsible choices that satisfy your values, your financial needs, and your tolerance for risk.

Student Loan Basics

Let's begin with the basics. When we talk about student loans, it often sounds as if we're talking about a single type of financial product. But just as with other consumer loans, there are multiple types of student loans, all with different features, advantages, and drawbacks. The first distinction that's important to appreciate is between government student loans, which are issued by the US Department of Education, and private student loans, which are issued by private banks just like mortgages and car loans. There are a number of important differences between private and government-issued student loans—namely the interest rates and benefits available to defer repayment when it's unaffordable—but they boil down to one general rule: don't take private debt if you can manage it. To see why, let's start with a quick primer on government loans.

Federal Student Loans

Pros: Low interest rates, generous safety net
Cons: Difficult to navigate

Students attending accredited colleges are generally eligible to borrow through federal lending programs. Loans issued by the government are (almost always) much cheaper and much safer than just about anything you'd find in a private loan marketplace—which is why federal student loans make up the vast majority (about 90 percent) of loans that are taken out each year.

The majority of federal student loans are issued through a program called the Stafford Loan Program. These loans are available to undergraduate students whose earnings and available assets are less than the total cost of their attendance. In the parlance of the financial aid officers and the Department of Education, Stafford loans are available to students on the basis of their "calculated financial need."

There are two types of Stafford loans, subsidized and unsubsidized (labels that are confusing at best and misleading at worst). Subsidized and unsubsidized loans differ in just one important way; interest on unsubsidized loans accrues while you're enrolled in school, whereas interest on subsidized loans does not begin to accrue until you've graduated. This makes a subsidized Stafford loan a better deal if you can get it. When you apply for financial aid, you'll be given an award letter indicating your eligibility for these and other types of loans.

Risk and Cost: Both types of Stafford loans have interest rates far below those offered by private banks or other third-party lenders. That's simply because the Stafford loan program is administered as a government program rather than a for-profit business. Whereas private lenders set interest rates higher in order to take a cut of every transaction, the interest rates for Stafford loans are set by policy, which means they can and do lose money year after year. At the time of writing, Stafford interest rates are set at 2.75 percent, compared to the up to 15 percent you could be charged by a bank. But since interest rates vary from year to year, you'll want to find the most up-to-date information on the website for the federal student loan program. (As always, make sure you're on a website that ends with ".gov" to make sure you're in the right place.)

Repayment: The interest rate savings on Stafford loans lower both the risk and the total cost of borrowing. But that's not the only way in which federal loans are less risky. When federal student loans first came about, they operated largely like private loans by imposing penalties in cases where a borrower couldn't afford to repay. But over the past decade, incremental policy changes that often occurred beneath the radar of the popular news cycle have ensured that every loan made through the Stafford program comes with a generous safety net. That safety net, also called income-driven repayment, is a set of federal programs that allow borrowers to pay only as much as they can afford each month without penalty, and to have their debt forgiven if their debt remains unaffordable in the long term. Borrowers don't get to decide what amount is affordable for them to pay; instead, each program has a formula that determines what is called "disposable income," and payments are set as a percentage of that number. When "disposable income" is low enough, borrowers aren't required to make any payments at all.

The definition of the "long term"—that is, the length of time after which a loan can be forgiven—depends on where the borrower is employed. When a borrower works for the government or a nonprofit, any balance that remains after their making income-based payments for ten years will be forgiven. Borrowers who work in the private sector, or don't work at all, will have to make payments for twenty years before they are eligible to have their debt forgiven.

In theory, these programs perfectly address the problem I've identified as central to our nation's challenge in higher education. They provide a form of insurance that ensures that a student borrower will not be financially ruined by their loan repayments even if their chosen investment in higher education doesn't allow them to land the job they were anticipating. In practice, however, there are a few kinks. First, the programs are tough to navigate. Unlike applying for federal loans, which is a relatively straightforward process, enrolling in reduced-payment plans takes close attention to detail paired with up-to-date knowledge of how the programs operate. For one thing, borrowers are automatically enrolled in repayment plans with flat monthly payments rather than payments that fluctuate with their ability to pay based on income. In order to make reduced payments without penalty you have to actively opt into a different repayment plan and go through the process of authorizing your income with the Department of Education through your loan servicer. Moreover, a misstep in repayment can cost a borrower big-time, as it may result in a loss of eligibility for loan forgiveness or a delay in benefits. However, I'm optimistic that by the time today's students start repaying their loans the system will have become more streamlined and user-friendly; the weaknesses of the current system are frequently brought to the attention of policy makers, and a movement for change is under way.

Eligibility/ How to Apply: There is a single application that all aspiring students should file in the year prior to their first semester of intended enrollment. It's called the FAFSA, or the Free Application for Federal Student Aid. It's a government form that requests information about your individual or family financial circumstances for the purpose of determining your eligibility for federal loans and grants. (Many states use the same application to determine eligibility for state-specific aid programs, so you should be mindful of specific deadlines in your state to avoid passing up any aid that you might be eligible for because of a late application.) Once you've completed the FAFSA, any college you're applying to (provided it participates in the federal financial aid program; most do) will be able to access the information on your application and use it to determine your financial aid award package, which generally gets delivered to you shortly following an acceptance. The award package will indicate any grants being offered to you by the school (including scholarships) and also indicate how much you are eligible to receive in Pell Grants and how much you are eligible to borrow in federal loans.

Filling the Gaps

What if you've made it to this point and find that the combination of cash on hand and your eligibility for grant aid and Stafford loans falls short of covering the cost? You still have a few options. First, if you're a dependent, your parents may be eligible to take out a type of federal loan, called a PLUS loan, in their name. But you should be aware that despite being government loans, PLUS loans don't offer anywhere near the protections that are offered on Stafford loans. And the interest rates on these loans aren't great either. Right now, they are at 5.3 percent, which is better than a credit card but worse than pretty much any other type of consumer loan available to borrowers with decent credit.

Private Loans
Cons: high interest rates, difficult to discharge in bankruptcy
Pros: can be useful for graduate and professional school

The last option, and one that should be used only as a last resort, is to borrow from a private lender. As I mentioned, private loans aren't inherently bad, just bad in comparison to the bargain that's being offered for federal student loans. The interest rates offered on private student loans can vary widely and are based on your ability to repay, your credit score, or even the credit-worthiness of your cosigner. Much as with mortgages or auto loans, the terms vary on the basis of the lender's assessment of you, and there's no guarantee you'll get one. In fact, they are probably least available to less well-off students, who pose a higher credit risk.

Taking on private debt to pay for a degree is putting a lot on the line. If you come up short when it's time to pay it back, you risk not only penalties and a tarnished credit score but also repossession of your car or garnishing of your wages. Further, private student loans are given special treatment in bankruptcy, but unfortunately, the special treatment is for the lenders, not for you. Student loans, both private and federal, are more difficult to discharge in bankruptcy than other types of debt (though federal loans are less likely to land you in that unenviable situation due to the option to use income-based repayment).

Private loans shouldn't be your plan A, but in certain situations they may need to be a plan B: for example, if you find yourself in the position of having exhausted your financial aid eligibility when you're just shy of completing your degree. Since the earnings needed to pay back that debt won't come until you've crossed the finish line, it could make sense to take on some private debt to make it happen if it isn't affordable otherwise. As with all debt, the key is to appreciate the risk you are taking and weigh it against the reward. In many situations there may be a better option, like enrolling at a cheaper school or lowering your living expenses to fit within the federal loan allowances.

One less risky use of private student loans is for graduate or professional school, particularly if your graduate degree will lead to greater future earnings. But even if it doesn't, students on that track are generally able to get private loans with interest rates that are somewhat competitive with federal loans. Since whether you graduate with your bachelor's degree is the number one predictor of whether you'll be able to pay back your loan, those already holding undergraduate degrees are given a better deal.

There's one more type of private student loan that is worth taking, but you won't need to think about it until after you've graduated. If you are on track to pay back your loans soon after graduation, you may find yourself eligible for private loan consolidation. These creditors make money by refinancing the loans of reliable borrowers who are unlikely to default on their debt. In other words, they pay back the federal loan on the borrower's behalf and issue a new loan to that borrower for the same amount but with a lower interest rate. They earn a profit by giving a slightly higher interest rate to the student borrower than the one they are paying on the cash they used to prematurely pay back the government.

It may sound a bit like a scam, but it really isn't. For many, maybe even most, eligible students, it's actually a great deal. This works just like mortgage refinancing. The lender is able to offer a lower rate than the one you have because interest rates in the market are below the current rate on your loan. It can be a win-win. If you find yourself paying back your loans with ease and don't anticipate having to rely on the safety nets afforded by federal loans, you could come out ahead by refinancing after graduation. On the other hand, if you find yourself unemployed or underemployed and struggling to make payments, you'd be trading in the terms on your federal loans for the terms on your new loan, which are likely less favorable, so you should pay close attention to the terms of your new deal before signing on the dotted line. Again, there's no right answer here. Whether giving up the protections offered by federal loans in exchange for a lower interest rate makes sense depends both on your expectations about what your professional future will bring and on your tolerance for risk.

Earnest and SoFi are two popular providers of student loan refinancing, but many other financial institutions, small and large, are also offering the service. If you choose to consider refinancing, whomever you choose to use should be carefully vetted. Unfortunately, the realm of student loan refinancing has attracted a number of scammers who try to take advantage of borrowers' confusion about their loan repayment options. I've received a dozen voicemails in just the past six months from supposed student loan financiers who have an offer to help me refinance my (no longer existent) student loans. Interestingly, the window for me to take advantage of their great offer is always "just about to close." In the best case, these scammers are simply going to charge you a fee to interact with the federal loan programs you're eligible to participate in for free. In the worst case, they have more nefarious ambitions.

The good thing is that student loan refinancing is something you can do at pretty much any point after you graduate. So if you're considering taking the step to lower your interest rate with this option, take all the time you need to do your homework. The extra cost you'll incur by paying a higher interest rate for a short time longer is minuscule compared to the potential cost of getting involved with a bad actor.

To Borrow or Not to Borrow

Now, I should warn you. What I'm about to suggest may sound crazy, especially if you've absorbed the message throughout your life that all debt is bad. But here goes. Even if you're in the fortunate position of not *having* to take out federal loans to pay for college, you may get a better deal by doing so than you would by paying cash.

To understand why I'm suggesting you take on debt even if you don't have to, let's return to the economic concept of "opportunity cost": the value of what you could be doing with the cash you would otherwise have used to pay for college.

Most people have a basic understanding of how interest on loans works: it is essentially the fee a borrower pays to be able to use money they don't have. But it's easy to forget, or not even realize, that using cash comes with a cost too. Instead of being charged the fee by someone else for using their money, the cost is in the form of the lost potential return on investment you give up by handing over your cash early. The same principle explains why keeping all your cash under the mattress isn't a wise proposition: because you're forgoing what that same cash could be earning if it was sitting in a savings account, or, better yet, invested in the market rather than just taking up space.

But how can that be true, when cash is free to use and loans charge interest? It's true because for most people the opportunity cost, the value of what you *could* be doing with your cash, is actually higher than what you'd pay in interest on a federal loan (given that those interest rates are unnaturally low; using private student loans instead of cash is seldom the right strategy for the reasons we've previously discussed).

At the time of this writing, federal student loan interest rates are approximately 3 percent. Let's suppose you have the cash to pay a $10,000 tuition bill but are also eligible to borrow that sum. If you were to invest that cash in the stock market and borrow to pay for school, you'd be paying the approximately 3 percent interest on the money you borrowed but earning double that from the return you'd likely see in the market (historically, the stock market has an average annual gain of 7 percent).

And that's a conservative scenario. If you took that cash and invested it in a retirement portfolio, likely returns would be even higher. Whether you have a 401k you could be contributing to or are able to open a Roth account, the tax benefits afforded to retirement savings mean that the return on retirement savings is often significantly higher than what is seen in the stock market. If you've got an employer match program that you aren't taking full advantage of, then you also have an extremely high-return investment opportunity that would offset the cost of borrowing several times over.

This isn't the only hidden cost incurred by choosing not to borrow. In 2015, two economists, Benjamin Marx and Lesley Turner, embarked on an experiment designed to help us understand how student debt affects academic and professional outcomes of borrowers. As it turned out, this seemingly simple question is incredibly challenging to answer. Normally, when we want to understand how one thing affects another, we'll run a controlled experiment. For example, when we want to know how a certain drug affects a particular health outcome, let's say blood pressure, we'll give the drug to one group of people and not another. Then we'll measure and compare the blood pressure of patients in each group. If the blood pressure falls only for those patients who took the drug, then we conclude that the drug worked to lower their blood pressure.

The analogous strategy for student debt would be to instruct one group of students to borrow and another to not. Then we'd measure a variable of interest (i.e., graduating, going bankrupt, buying a house, starting a family, etc.) and compare the outcomes of the two groups. The problem is that social experiments of this nature—that is, ones that can change the direction of people's lives in significant ways—are highly unethical. (Cue the sad trombone; womp womp.)

A simpler approach would be to compare outcomes of people who borrowed to outcomes of people who didn't borrow. But it doesn't take a PhD in economics to appreciate the shortcomings of this method. People who borrow to pay for college differ from people who don't in one very important way: they have less money. So it would be impossible to know which of these factors—having less money to begin with, or having taken on debt—to attribute to any given outcome.

So Turner and Marx partnered with a set of community colleges on a clever approach to uncovering this relationship. They couldn't force a random selection of students to borrow more to

pay for school. But they could encourage, or nudge, randomly se-
lected students to borrow more. Once they succeeded in doing
that, they could then follow the students through their college career and employ some fancy statistical techniques to parse out the
effect of student debt on their outcomes (like success in school
and work). And when they did, Marx and Turner found that the
students who had borrowed more earned higher grades and successfully transferred to four-year colleges at higher rates—both of
which would likely lead to opportunities for higher earnings and
a more robust return on their educational investment.

How did the researchers explain these results? Many students
who don't take on debt instead take on part-time jobs to help finance their schooling. Borrowing means less time spent at jobs,
which allows students to focus more intently on their studies, and
maybe even to enroll in more classes and graduate more quickly:
practices often associated with academic success and ultimately
higher earnings. Put another way, the students who chose not to
take on any loans paid an additional price in the form of extra time
spent enrolled and even the possibility of not finishing.

The second advantage of using debt over cash to pay for school
is that it gives you access, at almost no cost, to the very robust and
generous safety net discussed earlier. If you pay cash for your education, what you get is what you get. The price you paid will always be the price you paid, whether your degree pays off financially
or not. But with debt (again, we're only talking about government
debt here), the price you ultimately pay for that degree will depend
on whether it pays off financially or not. That's because if your
degree *doesn't* lead to the earning opportunities that make it worth
the price, you'll have access to those loan forgiveness programs
that essentially bring the cost of your degree down to a level more
in line with what it turned out to be worth. In other words, paying
with debt allows for the possibility of having the cost (to you) low-

ered retroactively in the case that your investment doesn't pay. In time, there will likely be markets for private college insurance that will accomplish this same thing, but in the meantime, borrowing is your best bet for mitigating the risk that the price you ultimately pay is out of line with the value you receive.

And there's one last reason why I'd advise aspiring college students to use government loans to pay for school, even when the cash is available. There has been ever-increasing chatter about the possibility that Congress will pass legislation that grants some sort of universal loan forgiveness or that it will even be done without congressional support through executive action. If you've paid out of pocket for school, you won't benefit from the additional security afforded by that sort of action. (The optimal strategy for individual students and their families is to maximize borrowing, but it's obvious that this isn't a great outcome from a social perspective. This is precisely why I've advocated against widespread loan forgiveness; it creates incentives for students to finance their education in ways that will ultimately be paid for by taxpayers, despite college graduates being better situated than the entirety of the tax base to afford the expense.)

Of course, borrowing won't automatically guarantee you a big payoff from college. But *not* borrowing—or not borrowing enough—can, in certain cases, stand in your way.

Student Loan Traps

In theory, borrowing to pay for your education makes perfect sense. In practice, however, there are a number of ways that you can get yourself off track. Most of the problems with student debt stem from a lack of information. So the best way to make sure you're on track is to pay careful attention. Easier said than done, I know. For better or worse, we have a system that makes taking out student debt pretty easy. That's great in the sense that it allows economically disadvantaged students to borrow what they need to enroll in college without getting caught up in red tape. But it's bad in that it allows students to wield a powerful financial tool without necessarily knowing what they're doing. Just as you wouldn't pick up a rotary saw without being pretty sure of how it works, you shouldn't pick up a student loan unless you're confident you understand the terms of the agreement you're signing and the protections that you can rely on if things don't turn out the way you imagined.

It might seem that the financial aid award letter you'll receive once you've applied for your financial aid (via FAFSA) and gotten accepted into a college would have all the answers, but it has a few shortcomings that you need to be aware of before you sign on the dotted line.

First, these financial aid award letters are notoriously difficult to parse. It's my job to understand how this all works, and I still find the language used on some financial aid award letters confusing. So I wasn't shocked when I read about one study that examined 515 letters and found 136 unique terms used to describe the unsubsidized Stafford loan, 24 of which didn't even include the word *loan*. The same study also found that a third of the letters failed to include key information on costs and that it was common practice for the letters to lump all sorts of financial aid into a single line so that it wasn't clear how much was in the form of grants (free money you don't have to pay back), loans (future money you do have to pay back), and work study (aid dollars paid out to students only in exchange for hourly work).

I'd like to give colleges the benefit of the doubt on this one, but it's hard to imagine a motive behind this lack of transparency other than trying to make aspiring students believe they are going to pay less than they really are. Either way, it's your job as the potential borrower to get to the bottom of what this letter is telling you: like how much of your aid is coming in the form of grants versus loans versus other types of aid that comes with strings attached like work study or even athletic or academic scholarships. And suffice it to say, that needs to happen before you've sealed the deal or mailed in your deposit.

Some helpful information on each of the different types of financial aid can be found on the website for the federal office of student financial aid (studentaid.gov). But if you still have questions, don't be afraid or embarrassed to call the financial aid office—repeatedly, if you have to. It's also important to understand that you can make your own decisions about how much to borrow. Financial aid offices have their hands tied on some dimensions of financial aid since eligibility rules are set by legislation, but they have flexibility in other ways. One such way is they get to decide how much debt to "package" in your financial aid award. This means that they can offer you as much or as little student loan money in that letter as they wish, up to the full amount you're eligible for. However, if you find that you don't really need the full amount you're eligible for, you're free to sign up for loans accordingly rather than as prescribed. This will mean talking to and working directly with your financial aid officer about your options. Pick up the phone or walk into their office to set up an appointment. As skeptical as I am of the incentives of colleges on the whole, I've never met a financial aid officer who didn't manifest genuine concern over the welfare of their students, especially the borrowers. Make use of that resource to be sure that you know where every dollar you sign for is coming from and going to.

Another Way to Pay . . . Is Not to Pay at All

Hopefully I've convinced you that loans aren't anything to be afraid of. But there is one even better way to pay, which is to not pay at all. Believe it or not, almost one-third of students enrolled in college today aren't paying *anything* to cover their tuition and fees. That's because they are taking advantage of a combination of state and federal grant aid that covers the entire expense.

Federal grants are funds that come from programs hosted by the Department of Education. Students who complete the Free Application for Federal Student Aid (FAFSA) will automatically be considered for a Pell Grant, which is essentially a cash gift from the government that goes toward reducing your cost of attending college. Pell Grants are awarded on the basis of financial need, which is determined by the costs you're facing relative to your ability to pay (based on the income and assets you report on the application). Those who demonstrate the highest levels of need will get the largest awards. For the 2020–21 academic year, the maximum award amount was capped at $6,345. The extent to which this covers your cost of enrollment depends, of course, on how expensive a program you've chosen to attend is. Even that full award would put only a small dent in a $50,000 per year price tag, but it might cover a year's tuition at a low-cost institution like a community college.

Things get a bit more confusing, but also more generous, when it comes to finding "free money" from state grant programs. Over the past decade, states and cities across the nation have taken some big steps in reducing the cost of higher education through an expansion of their grant programs or the creation of new ones. This was prompted, at least in part, by an aggressive initiative from the Obama administration to make college more affordable.

State and city programs now offer a huge number of unique grant programs that offer different sorts of benefits to students from their jurisdiction. Types of grant programs include academic achievement grants, financial need grants, and even grants that are specific to certain types of institutions, like community or four-year colleges. And some grants are even available to all without any eligibility requirements beyond residency.

The good news is that the existence of all these local grant programs can, for eligible students, subsidize the cost of school in a significant way. The bad news is that figuring out exactly how much you're going to have to pay, before you have to pay it, is more confusing than ever, since that financial aid letter detailing which grants you've been approved for comes so late in the game. So the best strategy is generally to apply for everything and anything you think you might be eligible for.

The best current resource for seeking grant dollars is a database hosted by the Graduate School of Education at the University of Pennsylvania in a program called Penn AHEAD (Alliance for Higher Education and Democracy). Visitors to their website can filter a search of the database by state to see the grant opportunities that are potentially available to them or use the clickable map to access the same information. The website provides basic information about program eligibility and for each grant offers a link to a website with more information about the time line and how to apply. This website should be a first stop for any aspiring student beginning to think about if, where, and how to go to college.

It's important to remember, however, that while grants might relieve the financial burden, they don't take all the risk out of the transaction. Even if grant dollars make your enrollment in college "free," there is still a tremendous cost of enrollment in terms of your time and in terms of what you could have earned or achieved in that time if you hadn't enrolled or had enrolled somewhere else.

The risk of spending years of your life on the wrong school or major still exists regardless of how much you pay to be there. So don't let free or discounted tuition and fees stop you from doing the analysis that we laid out in chapters 3 and 4. According to some recent research, a number of young people in Massachusetts learned this lesson the hard way.

In 2004, the state of Massachusetts introduced the Adams Scholarship, which reduced the cost of tuition at public colleges (but not private ones) for some high-achieving students in the state. When presented with a bargain they couldn't refuse, some students who would otherwise have begun their studies at selective private colleges enrolled at public colleges instead. The problem was, these public colleges had lower graduation rates, and many of the students in the study never finished their degree. Whether it was because of lower-quality instruction or because students adjusted their behavior to match that of their peers, those who *would* have completed a four-year degree in the absence of the scholarship ended up not completing any credential at all. According to the research authored by Joshua Goodman, distinguished economist and professor at Boston University, these students unwittingly reduced their chances of graduating by more than a quarter (27 percent). They simply didn't appreciate the trade-off they were making: a small discount for a big, and ultimately very consequential, reduction in quality.

The moral of the story is that the direct cost is only one piece of the cost-benefit analysis that should take place as you consider your options for enrollment. In the case of those students from Massachusetts, the appeal of "free" money lured them into the precarious position of trying to beat the odds at a lower-tier college rather than paying for an experience that would likely pay off for them in the long run.

No Free Money to Be Found?

If you find yourself ineligible for grant aid, whether from the Pell Grants program or a state program, consider yourself lucky. It's a sign that you're in a better financial position than many of your peers. If that's not enough of a consolation, allow me to explain why an expansion of state and federal grant programs to make college cheaper for you, or even free, would likely hurt you more than it would help.

First, you have to remember that free is never really free. Economists, especially conservative ones, often revel in being able to remind people of this fact and often do so using the annoyingly clichéd "There is no such thing as a free lunch." In other words, someone is going to be picking up the tab for all of these programs. And if you're not currently eligible for them, you're probably in a tax bracket that is effectively paying for them. So sure, we could expand program benefits to help all students pay for college, not just those with lower incomes, but if you're in that higher-income bracket, you'll basically be paying for your or your kids' education anyway (and possibly the education of other, even wealthier kids) in the form of higher taxes—all while adding to the cost of administering programs (requiring still higher taxes) and reducing the number of the choices available to aspiring students (since funds are often reserved for use at public colleges).

And there's another potential problem with expanding grant generosity at either the state or the federal level: it can result in increased prices that may completely erode the increase in purchasing power. That's because if colleges know their students have more money to spend, they may, in theory, raise prices. I know that we hate to think that our beloved colleges and universities would engage in that sort of behavior, but unfortunately, the market for higher education is just that—a market—meaning sellers (colleges) are incentivized to set prices at the highest level consumers (students) will tolerate. And that's especially true in a market like the one for college, where consumers (students) are "low-information" shoppers.

It's an idea called the Bennett hypothesis, after William Bennett, former secretary of education, who first put forth this argument in an op-ed for *The New York Times* during his time in office. Unlike Bennett, I don't believe that shaming colleges in the pages of national newspapers will solve the problem. And as an economist, I can't blame colleges for responding to the incentives put in place for them by policy makers. They aren't necessarily behaving in a predatory manner; after all, if they are performing a public service, then getting more money in their hands can only help them provide *more* of a public service, to more students. Regardless of their motives, pouring more money into subsidies for college, either through an increase in Pell Grants or through the introduction of new state scholarships that make college cheaper or even "free," will only exacerbate the existing problems in our higher education system and make college even riskier for tomorrow's students.

6

Insuring Your Investment

In the last three chapters I showed how information can be power when it comes to making decisions about if, where, and how to invest in a college degree. But after you've done your homework and developed strategies for avoiding the common pitfalls outlined in chapter 2, there is still plenty of uncertainty on the horizon. For example, you might find that the school you chose turns out not to meet your specific academic needs, or that the major you expected to enjoy studying has you pulling your hair out. Or you might find that the fast-paced legal career you'll spend years and hundreds of thousands of dollars preparing for will leave you crippled with anxiety and bedridden with migraines. Or perhaps you'll have the misfortune of graduating into an economic downturn, like the unlucky students graduating in the spring of 2020, who found themselves entering a job market unexpectedly and speedily devastated by the Covid-19 pandemic and the related closures. Unfortunately, there are plenty of reasons why even the most well-researched path through college won't pay off in the way you'd hoped. But the good news is that a number of strategies can help reduce the downside risk of putting all that money on the line when you invest in education after high school.

Before we get to those specific strategies, it's helpful to remember that we're all more used to managing risk than we tend to realize. Remember that risk simply means uncertainty about how one decision or another will pay off: something that's ubiquitous in all aspects of our daily lives, even if we aren't used to recognizing it as such. And we often use any number of techniques to protect ourselves from the downside risks of our everyday transactions.

For example, many products and services we buy come with some sort of satisfaction guarantee, especially big-ticket items like household appliances or cars, and high-cost services like tax preparation and moving. Businesses appreciate that the price of their product or service is large enough that the risk something will go wrong—the washing machine breaking the first time you use it, or your tax preparer making a mistake on your return that ends up costing you your refund, for example—is a primary concern for their customers. That's why they are often also in the business of selling money-back guarantees or warranties as a way to quell a customer's concern about the product or service not delivering what's expected. It's a dynamic that works well both for the customer, who might not be able to afford the risk that their purchase will turn out to be a lemon, and for the seller, who benefits from less anxious customers who are more willing to spend. Businesses also know that if the quality of the product they are selling is actually good, the cost of replacing the odd lemon here or there is minimal. What they are selling you when they ask if you want to tack a three-year warranty onto your purchase is peace of mind.

Guarantees are one tool that we've become accustomed to using to protect us from the risk of making a purchase that might not deliver. Another is insurance. We insure all sorts of things, from our homes and cars to items like that antique heirloom we inherited, or our most expensive jewelry. These days, pretty much anything with enough value that its loss would be acutely felt can be insured. Supermodels, celebrities, and star athletes have even been known to insure certain body parts: Rolling Stones guitarist Keith Richards, for example, reportedly insured his hands for $1.6 million, and Heidi Klum confirmed in 2011 that she had taken out a $2 million policy on her legs—relatively small sums compared to the $78 million insurance that soccer star David Beckham took out for his. And one "chocolate scientist" for the UK candymaker Cadbury even had her taste buds insured to the tune of $1.3 million, since "taste buds are incredibly important to her job."

The idea is that they'd be up a creek (or at least forced to move out of their Bel Air mansions) if these things suddenly stopped delivering for them. If Keith Richards broke one of his hands, he'd be unable to play guitar. If the chocolate scientist lost her sense of taste, she would no longer be able to "create new chocolate innovations" (arguably also a loss for society as a whole). And Heidi Klum, presumably, spends as though her legs will continue to make her money until the day she dies (or until they otherwise naturally "depreciate").

It might not be obvious what these examples could possibly have to do with your college education, but I promise the parallels are there. In each case, you have an expectation that something will continue to pay off for you over the long haul. In the case of college, we expect that the up-front cost of enrollment and forgone earnings for those years we're in school will pay dividends in the form of career and earnings opportunities over the course of our lifetimes.

You might be wondering why no one has ever told you that college tuition comes with the option of an insurance policy or money-back guarantee. The answer: historically, it hasn't, but times are changing fast, and opportunities to protect your investment are popping up all over the higher education landscape. They may not be marketed as "insurance" per se (or sold to you by a charming green gecko), but they are not all that hard to find as long as you know what you're looking for.

Meet Wade, Not Your Average Insurance Salesman

Wade Eyerly is a serial entrepreneur, and within a few minutes of meeting him you can tell he has a penchant for thinking big. He's also the founder and CEO of a company called Degree Insurance Corporation, which, as the name implies, sells insurance policies on college degrees.

Having grown up in a family of modest means, Wade appreciates that the primary goal of most aspiring college students is to eventually make more money. As he put it, rather charmingly, when we spoke, "Most of us are not eighteenth-century Regency period farmers just trying to better ourselves. Most of us go to college because we want to get better jobs."

But Wade isn't just a guy who wants to help college graduates get better jobs; he's also a businessman who views higher education as "the single largest uninsured investment market in the world." It's "the only place you counsel your loved ones to borrow five or ten times their net worth, make a single investment with it, and just hope it works," he says.

Wade's business is the first to offer a financial product designed and sold explicitly to protect students against the risk that their investment in higher education doesn't open the doors of economic opportunity for them after they graduate. Colleges and universities can buy an insurance policy on behalf of each of their students; those students who fail to land the sort of job that would make the tuition they paid worthwhile or find themselves earning below a predetermined threshold in the five years follow-ing graduation will be compensated with a lump sum check at the end of that period. (Unfortunately, schlepping off to Europe for five years won't be an option if you want that payout; you'll need to demonstrate that you're seeking full-time employment during that time.) It's a way for colleges to add value to the service they provide. Selling a $200,000 degree becomes an easier proposition when you can promise to deliver.

For Wade, this isn't just an untapped business opportunity (i.e., to insure the largest uninsured investment market in the world) but also a way of leveling the playing field. "The primary determi-nant of whether or not your degree makes sense—if it pays off—is the state of the macroeconomy in the year you graduate," he said, correctly. If betting on college is like spinning a roulette wheel, graduating during a recession is like landing on black: you've lost. For most students, that's the end of the story; when your chips are gone, you cut your losses and go home. But if you're rich, he ar-gues, you simply "double down" and spin again (i.e., go to gradu-ate school, or get an internship, or travel until the economy improves). Wade believes that insurance can help make that "sec-ond spin" a viable option for anybody.

Ensure the Future You Want

While Wade's vision for the future is still a ways off, the principles of insurance are already at work behind the scenes of some exist-ing programs.

Income share agreements (ISAs), for example, are a financial in-strument that students can use in place of (or in addition to) loans to finance the cost of going to college. Unlike loans, which are generally supposed to be paid back in increments on a predictable schedule, ISAs are repaid as a fraction of your future income.

Suppose you need $10,000 to cover the expenses of your enroll-ment but have maxed out the amount you are able to borrow from the federal loan program (which you should recall is always the cheapest and best option) and are on the fence between going to a private lender or taking advantage of the new ISA program being offered by your college or university. With the private loan, you'll be signing up to pay fixed monthly payments based on an amorti-zation schedule determined by your interest rate and other agreed-upon terms. In contrast, with an ISA you'll get that same $10,000 you need to pay the bills, but instead of repaying $200 a month (plus interest) for just over four years, you'll be expected to remit a percentage of your earned income for a predetermined number of months. In general, if you end up earning about what you (and the ISA financier) expected you to earn, your payments on an ISA will just slightly exceed those of a traditional loan. However, if you end up with lower earnings than you had anticipated, you will be on the hook for much less.

Now, this isn't exactly an insurance policy as you know it. But in the same way that health insurance protects you from having to pay for expensive medical care, the ISA protects you from having to face payments you can't afford.

Ten years ago, there were no ISA programs in operation in the United States. It was a wonky idea that existed only on the blogs of intrigued think tankers (i.e., me) and the pages of textbooks (it was once proposed by Milton Friedman, American economist and Nobel laureate best known for his strong belief in free markets). But over the past decade, a robust ISA marketplace has taken hold, with as many as sixty colleges and universities across the country now offering ISAs as part of their financial aid programs, includ-ing elite nonprofit colleges and large public universities. Most will have a fancy landing page for their ISA program right on the main college website. At the time of this writing, and likely for the foreseeable future, ISAs are available only through colleges themselves; there aren't any banks or other lenders offering them to customers.

If you are considering an ISA contract to supplement your arrangement for financing your enrollment, you'll want to pay close attention to details in your contract. This new financial product is unregulated (at the time of this writing) and terms can vary widely, including the generosity of the contract in the case that you aren't working at all. Taking a few years to roam Europe with a backpack might not get you out from under your obligation, since some contracts don't run the clock unless you are working.

Satisfaction Guaranteed!

I first became interested in the idea of money-back guarantees as a way of mitigating the risk inherent in higher education in 2015, at a meeting of Michigan Independent Colleges & Universities, which represents the state's private, not-for-profit colleges. After a presentation of my research on student loans, Jeffrey Docking, president of Adrian College, explained that his institution had launched a program that would help graduates make their student loan payments if they didn't land a high-enough-paying job after graduation. Specifically, graduates who earned less than $20,000 in annual income would have their entire loan payment covered by the college, and borrowers with annual incomes up to $37,000 would receive partial assistance.

The fact that Adrian students earn an average salary of about $39,000 a full ten years after graduation suggests that a nontrivial number of students would have been eligible for these benefits. This was an effort with some teeth.

I had already been writing and speaking about this notion of risk in higher education for some time and was thrilled to see someone taking a step that so explicitly tried to address what I saw as the core—but underappreciated—problem in the student loan market. I quickly learned that Adrian College was not alone in taking this step. Colleges were taking a page from every seller to ever appear on QVC by guaranteeing money back to any customer (student) for whom their product (a degree) didn't deliver a certain outcome, whether earnings, a job, or even the ability to graduate on time.

The genius of guarantee programs, when effectively designed, is that they put colleges on the hook to deliver what the aspiring students want or need. The guarantee means that both you, the student, and the college are working toward the same goal. Without guarantees, colleges have *some* stake in their students' success. If they consistently produce graduates who can't get jobs, their reputations will take a hit—a considerable liability in a marketplace where reputation is currency. If they consistently produce graduates who can't afford to pay their loans, they'll eventually lose federal funding. That all puts pressure on colleges to make sure their graduates have the means to pay back what they borrow.

But colleges with guarantee programs have even more on the line—and therefore even more of an incentive to help students succeed. They've made a contract to deliver exactly what the student wants, and failing to do so, even for a single student, means they'll pay a price. In practice that means colleges will be incentivized to build an infrastructure and business model that promotes student success rather than one that encourages application and enrollment. They'll be working for you. Best case, the result is better in-college experience and support in job placement than you'd have experienced otherwise. Worst case, they'll deliver you a payout that will hopefully make up at least some of the difference.

According to Peter Samuelson, president of Ardeo—the sole

provider of student loan repayment guarantee financing at the time of this writing—these sorts of income guarantee programs now exist at upwards of 140 colleges across the country, with that number growing by 25 percent annually. Colleges offering them tend to be private, nonprofit institutions with good student outcomes but less national name recognition. It seems they are using the loan repayment guarantees as a substitute for the confidence students feel from enrolling at a selective brand-name institution. Colleges with this type of guarantee program include Seattle Pacific University, Keystone College, and Cairn University, to name a few.

Most colleges with loan assistance repayment programs don't offer them broadly to all enrolling students; the guarantees are instead included in student financial aid packages to entice students to enroll who might not otherwise have done so. If a loan repayment assistance program is of interest to you, you'll need to inquire directly with the financial aid offices at the schools you're considering to see if it's an option; you might not be able to find it listed on their website as a benefit.

Some colleges and programs of study take a different approach by guaranteeing job placement instead of a certain level of earnings. This model is used at coding boot camps like Flatiron School and at traditional colleges like Thomas College in Maine. (We'll talk more about coding boot camps in the next chapter.)

If you're considering this sort of deal, you're going to want to read the fine print before you sign on the dotted line. You can't simply sit on your couch and enjoy having your loans paid off by one of these programs; the contract will require that you make a good-faith effort to find employment and prove that you did so by submitting evidence of job applications. The definition of "good-faith effort" varies by program but often entails applying for a certain number of positions and being willing to relocate and accept whatever jobs are available to you. Some critics have argued that the requirements are excessive and are intended to reduce the cost to the educational institution of providing the guarantee. Of course, reasonable people can disagree about what should be expected. But in any event, these programs aren't imposed on anyone, and if adequately informed up-front about their responsibilities, students can make their own decisions about the fairness of the terms.

When students fail to find qualifying employment, institutions compensate them in a few different ways. Some offer help paying back loans; others, such as Davenport University, offer continuing enrollment at no cost. Since institutions can't force employers to hire anyone, they can't truly guarantee employment. Instead, they offer other benefits aimed to make joblessness less costly or support students in their job search through benefits like continued enrollment and career counseling.

Are Guarantees Free?

Unfortunately not. Think about how new cars often come with some sort of narrow guarantee of service that can be extended for an additional cost. With college, the guarantee is usually baked into the price of tuition. Students don't know how much it's costing them because it's rolled into the overall cost of attendance, which covers a plethora of services from coursework to library access. In other cases, the guarantee is sold as an add-on. Either way, guarantees are never free.

You can expect to pay a bit more for a degree that comes with a guarantee because you are paying for someone else to bear the risk you don't want to take on yourself. You should think of this added expense as akin to the premium you pay for added certainty over your financial future. Insurance markets work because some entities, like financial institutions, can bear risk more readily than individuals. But they can't bear it without cost.

I've asked colleges about how much guarantee programs cost their students, but I'm always met with the same reply: they don't pass the costs on to students. That's a lovely idea, but it's almost certainly false. Even in cases where colleges don't pass the cost immediately through to their students in the form of a higher price tag, every dollar they spend on guarantee programs means one less dollar to spend on other aspects of the students' experience. One only hopes that colleges cut back on expenditures like lawn fertilizer rather than library books, but college finances are largely a black box, and following the money in this case would be a lost cause.

But the point stands that guarantees aren't free. It costs colleges to provide them, and in a competitive marketplace that cost gets passed on to students, one way or another. Whether guarantees become commonplace in higher education will depend on just one thing: whether a critical mass of students dislike risk enough that they're willing to pay a higher price to avoid it. If so, we'll likely see guarantees and the accompanying marketplace grow. If not, this will continue to operate as a niche market.

The Federal Loan Safety Net

In addition to the smattering of college-specific guarantee and insurance programs we now see in operation around the country, all students who use federal student loans to pay for their education are being given a form of insurance, whether they realize it or not.

As discussed in chapter 5, all federal student loans administered by the US Department of Education come with an option to repay based on income. The programs that allow borrowers to do that are essentially offering a guarantee that the student will never face a monthly payment on their loan that exceeds an affordable share of their disposable income. Since these programs also offer loan forgiveness after a period of time, they also guarantee that the student will be off the hook completely (excluding any tax obligation) in twenty years, regardless of how their finances shake out in that time. These programs were born out of public concern over the plight of students who borrow and ultimately find repayment to be unaffordable on the basis of how much they earn.

These programs are often classified as a safety net, akin to food stamps or welfare, but they are really just part of the terms of your loan. Essentially, by financing your education in whole or in part by federal student loans, you're taking out an insurance policy on your education. Federal loans allow you to defer the up-front cost of enrollment and protect you from sinking deeper into debt in the case that your degree doesn't pay, even if it's because you don't graduate or for some other reason that is entirely within your control.

Why It's Risky to Be an Optimist

If you don't think you need these kinds of protections, you're in good company. To better understand the way students feel about the risk inherent in going to college, I conducted some focus groups to talk with students (aspiring, current, and former) about the concept of insuring their investments in higher education. Interestingly, participants who were still working toward their degree mostly said they didn't see a need for insurance; they were confident in their ability to find a good-paying job. Those who had already graduated, on the other hand, thought it sounded like a great idea. It seems that the experience of having looked for their first job had lowered their confidence about their future job prospects.

Optimism about the future is generally something to be encouraged. But it can also be a barrier to broad adoption of risk-mitigating strategies like the ones discussed in this chapter. And college students are notoriously optimistic about their economic futures. For example, when colleges and servicers talk to students about ISAs, students seem to have an inordinate level of concern for the possibility that they'll hit it big and end up paying back much more than they used in the first place. According to someone familiar with the financial modelling for ISA pricing, servicers are more than willing to include repayment caps to quell student concerns because the risk to them of doing so is very low: that is, the number of students who expect to hit it big exceeds the number who actually do so, by a wide margin.

So the answer to the question "Do I really need a guarantee?" is, of course, "It depends." Risk is not a universal experience; it depends on each student's personality and, perhaps more important, on their financial circumstances. For example, students with a large trust fund or family wealth would probably see no reason to pay an additional cost to insure their college education, as their financial safety net would make them more resilient to poor employment or earning outcomes. On the flip side, students supporting themselves and perhaps even a family might not have the luxury of rolling the dice when it comes to college. While mitigating the risk of your investment in higher education is a notion that makes good theoretical sense, it's up to you to gather the necessary information and weigh the costs and benefits relevant to your individual situation.

7

Unbundling Your Education

The way we talk about college education in this country makes it easy to forget that the notion of "a degree" is completely manufactured. There's no natural law designating four years as a standard unit of education. The traditional model of education in this country and across much of the world is built on arbitrarily designed building blocks of educational achievement. Is it really conceivable that four years of full-time study are precisely the appropriate amount of training and preparation for *every* job requiring a college diploma? I don't think so. More likely, employers have come to rely on this standard measure of achievement because it saves the trouble of having to assess disparate collections of educational experiences across all of their job candidates. It is far simpler to have just one standard that aspiring employees must achieve.

These strict definitions of education have become so ingrained in our culture that it's hard to imagine otherwise. The movement advocating for universal access to postsecondary education is (regardless of your politics on the issue) just one of many stark examples of how reflexively we celebrate this model and how reflexively we reject, at least implicitly, the idea that postsecondary education can take new and different forms.

But of course it can. Alternative models of education have always existed in this country and have succeeded in ushering generation after generation of workers into productive roles in our workforce. For example, electricians often receive training through apprenticeships, the time-honored tradition in which workers become eligible for a license to practice their trade independently only after they've worked a specific number of hours shadowing a licensed practitioner. No course credits are awarded along the way. Students don't live on a campus with a well-manicured lawn or join a fraternity. But they do receive an education—one that lands them in a stable career. It works for them and their families because it all but guarantees gainful employment and a steady income stream. And it works for our society, which benefits not only from their expertise but from those individuals thriving and contributing to their community.

It works because it boils the notion of "education" down to what it is fundamentally about: the development of skills. Those skills can range from the specific, like how to write computer code, to the general, like how to think creatively to solve a unique problem.

There is another aspect of the traditional all-or-nothing model of higher education that creates unnecessary risk for students: the disconnect with the labor market. While the primary mission of most students enrolling in college is to gain access to a well-paying career, the mission of most colleges is, as Harvard University puts it, "to educate the citizens and citizen-leaders for our society." Since Harvard (like higher education in general) has historically succeeded in helping graduates land jobs that earn them more money, it seems that there is some overlap between what it takes to be a good citizen and what it takes to be a good employee. But the explicit mismatch in motives is troubling, especially for students who lack access to the professional network afforded to or inherited by students attending selective colleges like Harvard. For these students, skills are what matter.

Fortunately, a growing number of new and nontraditional options for education after high school—let's call them college alternatives—are closing this gap by partnering with employers to give students a direct pathway from classroom to career. This relationship not only supports job placement but gives employers a hand in the development of the curriculum to ensure that graduates are acquiring the specific skills that will make them desirable prospects for hiring managers after graduation. When this model works as it should, students needn't gamble on whether the package of skills and knowledge they acquire in becoming a "citizen-leader" of society will also land them a job that pays the bills.

Unbundling Your College Experience

For the last two years there has been an ongoing battle in my household. I, the pragmatic, penny-pinching millennial, am in the camp advocating to "cut the cord"—that is, replace our cable television package with some à la carte channels, like Disney+ (for the kiddo) and NBA League Pass (to watch our beloved Utah Jazz) to complement our existing subscription to Netflix. My husband, on the other hand, does not. I argue (correctly) that we could save money every month if we were to ditch the bundle of services provided by our cable provider and replace it with a slimmed-down collection of individual services that we actually use, but he isn't ready to make the switch. To me, the economics are simple: the bundle makes some sense for TV addicts who routinely consume programming across many of the gazillion available channels, but it's highly inefficient for families like us who end up paying for things that we don't need or even want.

A similar dynamic is at play with higher education. With the traditional, prevailing model, colleges and universities are essentially offering a bundle of services, just like the cable provider. When a student enrolls in the typical bachelor's degree program, they are generally signing up and paying for a whole host of services all at once. Yes, your tuition check buys the opportunity to attend courses, engage with faculty, and earn credits. But it also grants you access to the libraries, the fitness center, and other on-campus resources like career counseling, the writing center, and health services. And those are just the basics! At some schools, your tuition gives you access to tennis courts, Olympic-sized swimming pools, rock walls, movie screenings and lecture series, or, if you enroll at the University of Iowa, a leisure pool with a "lazy river" feature—all of which you are stuck paying for, whether you use those amenities or not (just as I'm stuck paying for the Hallmark Channel and the Home Shopping Network, but I digress).

There are certain advantages to bundling education in this way. Some even argue that an immersive education (one that includes floating down the lazy river, apparently) is all part of the magic of college. But I tend to think that this argument has been overused to justify the ever-escalating cost of attendance. We think of the "package" of services as defining the quintessential college experience. But by bundling all of those services together, we are also making college riskier than it needs to be.

These all-inclusive models of higher education have for a long time so dominated the marketplace that aspiring students wishing to pay "à la carte" only for those amenities and resources they actually use will have limited options. Fortunately, change is on the horizon.

Covid-19 Strikes a Blow to the Status Quo

In the spring of 2020, the Covid-19 pandemic delivered a serious blow to higher education in the United States. Hit hardest were the colleges that had previously capitalized on delivering the "all-in" experience of college that's often portrayed in the movies: tailgating at football games, long hours with study buddies in the library, dorm living (and dorm partying), enriching banter with faculty in between classes, and so on. All of these activities, which had been sold as a critical complement to the basic academics being taught in class, had to be put on hold. It turns out the very same activities that purportedly spread self-discovery and knowledge also spread the respiratory particles that can infect a person with Covid-19. The result was that colleges across the country had to shutter their campuses, sending students home to wherever they came from, and causing faculty to scramble to move their courses online.

Two young entrepreneurs, having finished college only somewhat recently themselves, saw this moment as an opportunity rather than an obstacle. Lane Russell and Adam Bragg appreciated that students who had previously been paying for an all-inclusive college experience wouldn't be eager to pay the same or just slightly reduced tuition to spend the next year (or more?) taking online courses and missing out on the in-person aspect of college. Their solution: the U Experience.

The U Experience, as initially conceived, aimed to provide a better substitute for the social experience of being on a college campus. They rented out entire hotel properties and planned to set up "bubble-like" learning environments where residents could tend to their online coursework but also have the opportunity to socialize with a cohort of other students, all while observing Covid-19 testing and prevention protocols similar to the ones successfully employed by the NBA during the 2020 playoff season.

For the (not-so) low price of just $10,500, residents of these learning bubbles would enjoy a private room and bathroom, daily breakfast, a pool, gym membership, and all the nasal swab tests their heart desired (and if their Instagram account is any indication, the company of several bikini-clad co-eds would also be provided).

The response wasn't entirely positive. On the Twittersphere and elsewhere, many likened their venture to the now-infamous Fyre Festival scam (lest you have forgotten, that was the fraudulent luxury music festival that had attendees eating prepackaged sandwiches rather than the promised gourmet meals and sleeping in FEMA tents rather than the promised luxury villas). And their initial plan, to operate at multiple locations, was cut down to size when local officials opposed their bringing these potential Covid-19 hotbeds into their communities. Last I checked, the petition to stop the U Experience was just shy of fifteen thousand signatures. It turns out that a business model based on bringing together people from far-flung parts of the globe in a time when public officials were telling—no, begging—us to keep our social distance would be an uphill battle.

And yet, while the pandemic may have doomed their company from the beginning, it may also have been the opening they—and other like-minded entrepreneurs—needed to be able to break the traditional model of higher education wide open. As college students around the country found themselves taking virtual classes from their childhood bedroom for the price of an in-person college experience, many were starting to think a bit more deeply about what exactly they were paying for and whether there might be a better way.

I believe Russell and Bragg are on to something, even if the current pushing against them ultimately proves too hard to withstand. When I spoke with them about their business and their plans for the future, they made clear that this wasn't a get-rich-quick-from-Covid scheme they had cooked up overnight. Instead, they seemed to have a pretty keen understanding about the landscape of higher education and some pretty smart ideas about how it could be disrupted to better serve our nation's students. They saw a future in which students needn't buy all aspects of their educational experience in one stop. Instead, students who preferred online and virtual learning over a classroom but who also valued the social experiment of college could create a kind of hybrid experience that better suited their needs. I don't know if the U Experience will survive the month, let alone the year. But I'm pretty sure that the trend they were hoping to exploit—the unbundling of higher education, and the option to customize your own experience and pay only for the extras you want and need—is here to stay.

Coding Boot Camps

Early last year, on a monthly business trip to Manhattan, I had the chance to sit down with a reporter for a major national newspaper who covered higher education, among other things. As we sipped our cups of coffee in a bustling corporate cafeteria with an impressive view of Midtown, I began running through my semi-rehearsed spiel about the research projects I'd been working on and issues I'd been otherwise following. When I got to the part about how I was excited to be following the emergence of new business models in higher education, she interrupted me to ask: "You mean boot camps? But aren't those just scams?" Her earnest question, prompted by the fact that a friend had recently asked for her opinion regarding the possibility of enrolling their son, made me laugh—not because it was a dumb question, but because it was such a vivid example of how our bias for the traditional four-year degree education leads us to reject new alternatives out of hand. And in case you are wondering: no, boot camps are not in fact a scam.

Over the past six years, an entire industry around boot-camp-style postsecondary education has sprouted and taken hold. In the context of education, a boot camp can (as the name implies) be broadly characterized as a high-intensity, short-duration path to mastering a skill or subject—a strictly or at least mostly measurable skill–based training program that strips away the bells and whistles typically bundled together with skill development. This model, despite having only recently come into existence, is already proving successful in landing students in high-paying jobs.

In 2012, the first boot camp, Bloc, opened its doors, enrolling students in a $3,000 software developer program that offered a personalized curriculum based on content it had previously made available as part of its free, open-access courses. This arrangement served as a model for the many other programs, mostly focusing on coding, that soon followed. While the total size of the boot-camp industry is tricky to measure because it is largely unregulated and somewhat heterogenous, industry reports suggest that boot camps are now a $240 million industry with 108 programs graduating upwards of twenty thousand students per year. Student outcomes are also challenging to measure, but an industry report, albeit based on a limited number of programs, suggests that 80 percent of students are placed into jobs related to their training within 180 days with starting salaries averaging over $70,000. Not bad for a program that lasts an average of fourteen weeks and costs about $12,000.

One interesting fact is that among the current crop of boot-camp students, the vast majority are taking these innovative courses of study after already completing a traditional degree.

This suggests that the industry is picking up the slack in a space where traditional higher education may be falling short.

The open question, however, is how durable these skills will be in the long term. Those with college degrees generally see their earnings potential increase over time, likely because their training is sufficiently general to allow them to adapt to evolving technologies in the labor market. Time will tell whether the narrowly focused training programs employed in boot camps will yield the same durability for their graduates or if this style of education demands that workers return to schooling periodically throughout their lifetime to reskill for the evolving marketplace. The latter is not necessarily worse. In fields where innovation happens quickly, such as computer programming, it's already common practice for employers to provide their staff with funds to use for coursework to keep up with the cutting edge. And someone who enrolled in three boot-camp programs at a price tag of $12,000 each over the course of their career would end up spending less than half what they would have paid for the typical four-year degree.

There is one catch, however: for the most part, boot camps operate outside the system of federal accreditation, which means that students are unable to access dollars from the federal student aid program in the form of grants or loans. It means that these programs face a financial challenge above and beyond the one faced by traditional institutions. They stay in business only if their students are willing to pay the full cost of enrollment out of pocket—though some boot camps have been savvy enough to employ a financing model that reduces the risk to students of doing so: income share agreements.

As that reporter's skeptical comment suggests, however, enrolling at a new, untested educational program like a boot camp is risky. What would give the students the confidence to fork over several thousands of dollars to a relatively untested model? That's where the income share agreements come in. Some boot camps allow students to pay the entire cost of enrollment by sharing a fraction of their future earnings. Instead of paying a price upfront, they pay only if they land a job with a salary above a certain threshold after graduation. This also serves to align the mission of the program with that of the student: to land them a high-paying job.

Getting Credit for What You Know

Another growing category in the postsecondary education marketplace is competency-based education (CBE). With the traditional higher education model, students sit through a predetermined curriculum, demonstrate mastery of those topics through credit completion, and then enter the labor market with a credential in hand. College as we know it serves two functions. First, it imparts skills; students learn how to do things, or think about things, in a way that is valuable to their future employers. This is what we often think of as being the primary value proposition of higher education. But a college degree is valuable in another, perhaps more important way as well: it provides a stamp of approval that a student can bring with them into the workforce to indicate to employers what skills they possess (or, to look at it more cynically, what educational curriculum they have sat through).

Competency-based education takes a completely different tack. This model presumes, at least implicitly, that skill attainment is measurable. It also recognizes that the credential is often the thing employers pay attention to when making hiring decisions, rather than the skill itself. And it allows students to obtain both skills *and* credentials, on an à la carte basis, rather than through a predetermined curriculum. In the end, students walk away with a credential comparable to degrees earned in a traditional manner; CBE graduates may hold associate's and bachelor's degrees or earn any number of professional certifications.

CBE students progress through a series of examinations designed to measure whether they have mastered a particular skill. Coursework is available to explicitly support that endeavor. If a student can demonstrate mastery of a skill without ever sitting in a classroom, they will be granted the appropriate credential without having to sit through (and pay for) a class just for the sake of doing so. In CBE programs, education is a means to an end; as long as a student can show they've attained proficiency in a skill or subject, the CBE provider could care less how they attained it.

Students progress through CBE programs at their own pace rather than on a predetermined academic calendar. Rather than having to sit in a seat for an entire semester and play along with homework assignments, quizzes, and class participation, students in CBE programs are given access to learning materials and can choose to take a test to prove their competency at any point in time. Students with skills developed before enrollment could progress through the program at breakneck speeds because they wouldn't need to waste time learning something they already know. As you'd imagine, this is a model that works well for older aspiring students who have developed skills through working but don't have the right credential to prove it.

The growth in CBE programs has been slow, but also deliberate, to ensure that growth wouldn't come at the expense of quality. While there is no national database of CBE programs, a 2019 survey of postsecondary institutions indicated that 11 percent of US institutions had at least one full CBE program in operation, while another 51 percent reported being in the process of adopting CBE. Even pre-Covid-19, many of these programs were offered virtually, making CBE an option for students all over the country despite their operation in a relatively small number of institutions. If you're looking for a CBE program, you might want to check with colleges on your list to see if it's something they'd offer. Or simply do a web search for CBE programs in the field you intend to study. Major CBE providers such as Western Governors University, Purdue Global, and Southern New Hampshire University's College for America are sure to pop up on the first page of your search engine results (even if they show up as sponsored links, don't write them off as a scam; this kind of advertising is not how traditional colleges do business, but it's common practice in more entrepreneurial realms of the higher education marketplace).

These programs are generally geared toward students with some experience under their belt who are looking for a faster pathway toward a degree. You'll be most likely to find CBE programs in the fields of nursing and health professions, computer and information sciences, and business administration, though I'd expect that field to widen in the years to come.

While traditional education may still be the best path for many, we can recognize that alternative modes like boot camps or competency-based education provide another pathway to employability and financial prosperity. But just because CBE comes with a fancy moniker, the economics isn't any fancier. You still want to do your homework in the same way when considering your options. Compare the up-front cost against the expected reward, based on how other students before you have fared after graduation.

Getting Employers to Pay

When a student receives financial aid for a portion of their tuition with grants or loans, they are essentially sharing the financial cost with taxpayers. Both state and federal subsidies, combined with the student's own dollars (sometimes in the form of their future dollars) are what pay the bills that enable colleges to keep their lights on and enable individual students to enjoy the benefits of enrollment. But recently, employers have been taking on a growing responsibility in sharing some of the risk that previously sat entirely on the shoulders of students, while also lifting some of the burden on taxpayers.

The notion of employers paying for their workers' education is not entirely new. We used to hear a lot about companies offering tuition subsidies for employees who earned advanced degrees while working. And companies have always had and will always have to train workers in the specific skills necessary to do their jobs. But employer-pay models are emerging in new forms that may alleviate the financial burden for their future employees before they enter the workforce.

For example, we're seeing more and more businesses partnering with colleges or vocational schools to help arm future workers with the skills they need to seamlessly enter the workforce, often by offering opportunities for paid apprenticeship training while students are still in school. In fact, there is enough demand for this type of program that a small industry of apprenticeship brokers has emerged. Companies like Techtonic, Vendition, Dev Degree, and LaunchCode offer training and apprenticeship programs that are designed to prepare workers for placement into jobs (though students are generally hired at the end of their program, job placement isn't guaranteed). Because the brokers have relationships with the employers, the curriculum is designed to meet their specific needs. The employer covers some or all of the expense of enrollment, and in return they get to hire appropriately skilled employees already trained and ready to hit the ground running. In the case of Vendition, a three-month tech sales apprenticeship program, students receive a monthly living stipend of $2,500.

This movement may be in response to a growing sense among

employers that skilled labor is exceedingly difficult or even impossible to find. In surveys, hiring managers often report that traditional higher education is not equipping students with the skills they require for employment. The problem seems to span all sectors of employment, including the trades, middle-skilled jobs, and high-skilled STEM jobs. In a 2019 survey, 83 percent of human resource professionals reported that they'd had difficulty recruiting suitable job candidates in the last twelve months. At the same time, there are reportedly seven million unfilled jobs in the US economy. Clearly, this is an area where change is sorely needed.

While the innovations in this space are being driven by employers seeking to enhance their bottom line, they aren't the only ones who benefit. The employer-pay model reduces the risk for students in two ways: it reduces their out-of-pocket investment in education, and it increases the odds of that education leading to a well-paying job. In essence, students get paid to learn. It's the employer who's gambling that the spending will pay dividends for their business. And since employers have a diversified portfolio of investments, they are far better equipped than individual students to absorb this risk.

Critics of this model often worry that the skills students obtain through it won't serve them well in the long run. They argue that with the traditional style of education students are gaining a skill set general enough that they'll be employable across many jobs, companies, and even industries, rather than just the specific one for which they have been groomed. There's also a concern that the acquired skills in these sorts of programs won't be durable, possibly expiring with the introduction of the latest technology.

I am optimistic that students gaining employment through these channels will not face limited employment or earnings opportunities relative to traditionally trained students. The "problem" of specialization is not unique to these workers, since traditionally educated workers also end up specializing in the skills utilized by their employers. And the need to reskill as technology evolves is universal. I'd contend that students resourceful enough to find, enroll in, and complete these innovative programs have already demonstrated more of an ability to adapt to changing labor market circumstances than those who follow the same educational path that students have taken for hundreds of years.

The benefits of these sorts of arrangements are vast—and still remain largely untapped. According to research from the Center on Education & Skills at New America, "Apprentices today are overwhelmingly white and overwhelmingly male, meaning those who reap the rewards of apprenticeship don't reflect the diversity of Americans who could benefit." In other words, those who have the least access to traditional higher education, because of the financial cost and risk, have yet to be served by this new employer-pay model, despite the early indications that alternative education providers may better serve disadvantaged students.

A New Landscape of Options for Students

So far, the new models described in this chapter are most often employed in technology-related fields, where the skill set required for employment is tangible and easy to measure. The question that remains is whether these models can work as effectively in a wider array of fields. Just because we don't yet know how they will work doesn't mean that they can't. Certain models may be adopted more easily in certain realms of education than in others. But in reality, should the different fields of study and employment all follow the same educational model? They shouldn't. So perhaps what we are seeing isn't a reinvention of education but rather a diversification.

8

Oh, the Places You'll Go

You have brains in your head. You have feet in your shoes.
You can steer yourself any direction you choose. You're
on your own. And you know what you know. And YOU are
the one who'll decide where to go.

—Dr. Seuss

The seven chapters you just read offered a pragmatic, even
mathematical, way of thinking about decisions regarding
education after high school. This practice of boiling a problem
down to the measurable, nonsubjective components is what economists do. But we aren't so foolish as to believe that this approach
doesn't miss something too.

For me, college was first a means to an end: financial independence. But it also delivered me into a career that I love. Through
college I accomplished my goal of being able to pay my rent, cover
groceries, and still have enough in the bank to save a little each
month. But I also accomplished much more; I was able to find my
calling, a career that brings a smile to my face most days and provides me with immeasurable intrinsic reward.

I expect that college will be much more than a means to a financial end for you. And those intangible returns will only be

sweeter when the financial foundation you've built for yourself is sound.

You may have noticed that this book is largely lacking in specific recommendations on exactly where to go, what to study, how much to pay, and why. Plenty of existing resources—books, lists, and rankings—do the job of sharing the author's ideas about the best path for you. Instead, what I hope you were able to take away from this book is a clearer way of thinking about how to make *your own* decisions about college, a way to make decisions that maximizes the likelihood that the path you choose will lead to wherever you want it to. I don't claim that this advice is 100 percent foolproof. But I promise that it's the same I'd give my son today if he were old enough to be considering such things.

While the specifics of the various strategies discussed in these chapters will likely change over time, the principles that underlie them will remain the same, and therefore are worth recapping in brief:

Know what you want to achieve and why you want to achieve it. Getting a handle on your goals, your constraints, and your non-negotiables *before* you begin shopping for college is probably the single most important aspect of the process.

Appreciate the trade-offs that you're facing. A common decision-making mistake is putting too little consideration into "what could have been." Evaluating your options for college and beyond without comparing realistic alternatives can lead you astray. Recognizing the trade-offs involved in these options is critical to making decisions that pay.

Appreciate the risk, as well as the price, of investing in education. Because the debate about college is so focused on the price tag, it's easy to forget that risk should be a primary consideration of whether one path is preferable to us over another. Remember that price is just one side of the cost-benefit analysis that can determine whether your college career will pay off. A high price tag that delivers certain returns is in a sense a "cheaper" option than a lower-priced path that is riddled with risk.

If you use nothing else but these four principles to guide your decision-making, I'm confident that you'll succeed in making college pay.

Appendix: Resources

Throughout the book I've referred you to a number of resources to assist in your college search. To save you the trouble of bookmarking them, I'm providing a review of them here.

College Scorecard
collegescorecard.ed.gov

The College Scorecard is the holy grail of information on earnings after graduation for every major at every college in the country. It also provides that ever-important graduation rate and reports the average annual net cost that students pay (including room and board and taking into account grants and scholarships).

The College Scorecard is hosted online by the US Department of Education and is a free resource. To be sure that you've landed on the right website, check to see that your URL ends with ".gov." Unfortunately, many private entities seek to make money off of the complexity of the college application and financial aid process, and they sometimes do so by mimicking official websites.

PayScale College Return on Investment Report (ROI)
payscale.com/college-roi

PayScale is another high-quality source of information about how much students earn after graduating from different colleges and majors. Unlike the College Scorecard, which reports earnings in the first year after graduation, PayScale also provides indications of later-life earnings, including early-career salary (one to four years of experience), mid-career salary (ten-plus years of experience), and an estimated twenty-year ROI. At the time of this writing, this information is available without charge on the company's public website.

College Navigator
nces.ed.gov/collegenavigator

The College Navigator is another official website that provides a directory of all colleges eligible to participate in the federal student aid program. On the homepage you'll find a search tool that will allow you to narrow your search on many dimensions, including state, zip code, major, institution type (public, private nonprofit, or private for-profit), tuition, enrollment, standardized test scores, sports, and others. The College Navigator is a great place to start if you're working from your list of non-negotiables or "must-haves" and need to develop a list of schools to consider more carefully. The College Navigator is hosted by the National Center for Education Statistics at the US Department of Education. Like the College Scorecard, this is a free governmental resource.

The Economic Value of Majors Report
cew.georgetown.edu/cew-reports/ valueofcollegemajors

These estimates on earnings across different majors, which are referenced in chapter 4 and included as a table in the Appendix, are referenced from a report published by the Center on Education and the Workforce at Georgetown University, called *The Economic Value of Majors*. Along with the report, the center has published additional reader tools that can help you explore this data further, including an option to examine earnings by major within specific states. If you're undecided on a major and wish to consider earnings trends in your decision-making, a stop at this website would be worthwhile. The report and related tools are hosted on the website for Georgetown University.

Free Application for Federal Student Aid (FAFSA)
FAFSA.gov

When it comes time to pull the trigger on college applications, you'll also want to go ahead and submit the Free Application for Federal Student Aid (FAFSA) to begin the process of learning about your eligibility for federal student aid, including student loans. Even if you think that your income or wealth (or combination thereof) will make you ineligible for federal student aid, you may need to complete this application anyway to be considered for aid from the college or state. You can find the FAFSA online at the website for federal student aid at the Department of Education. There you will also find a schedule for when the FAFSA is due in each state. Deadlines at colleges may also vary, so the best approach is to complete this step early to ensure that you don't miss the boat on aid for which you'd otherwise have been eligible.

College Promise Program Database, PennAHEAD
https://www.ahead-penn.org/creating -knowledge/college-promise/

This is a searchable database of grants and scholarships with geographic eligibility constraints that are available to aspiring college students.

Earnings by Major

*(Reprinted with permission from the
Georgetown University Center on Education and the Workforce)*

Detailed Major	Annual Salary		
	50th percentile	25th percentile	75th percentile
All Bachelor's Degree Holders	$59,000	$40,000	$88,000
Agriculture and Natural Resources	$54,000	$38,000	$80,000
Animal Sciences	$48,000	$33,000	$73,000
General Agriculture	$52,000	$36,000	$79,000
Plant Science and Agronomy	$52,000	$36,000	$75,000
Miscellaneous Agriculture	$54,000	$40,000	$80,000
Natural Resources Management	$54,000	$40,000	$77,000
Forestry	$61,000	$45,000	$83,000
Agricultural Economics	$65,000	$42,000	$98,000
Food Science	$67,000	$42,000	$99,000
Architecture and Engineering	$80,000	$57,000	$109,000
Architecture	$65,000	$45,000	$93,000
Engineering Technologies	$65,000	$43,000	$95,000
Mechanical Engineering–Related Technologies	$65,000	$47,000	$89,000
Biomedical Engineering	$68,000	$44,000	$96,000
Miscellaneous Engineering Technologies	$69,000	$48,000	$94,000

Detailed Major	Annual Salary		
	50th percentile	25th percentile	75th percentile
Industrial Production Technologies	$70,000	$50,000	$97,000
Environmental Engineering	$73,000	$57,000	$98,000
Miscellaneous Engineering	$73,000	$52,000	$101,000
Engineering and Industrial Management	$75,000	$52,000	$110,000
Engineering Mechanics Physics and Science	$77,000	$50,000	$111,000
General Engineering	$78,000	$52,000	$105,000
Architectural Engineering	$78,000	$55,000	$105,000
Industrial and Manufacturing Engineering	$79,000	$55,000	$106,000
Civil Engineering	$80,000	$60,000	$105,000
Mechanical Engineering	$84,000	$63,000	$111,000
Aerospace Engineering	$88,000	$63,000	$115,000
Mining and Mineral Engineering	$90,000	$53,000	$126,000
Electrical Engineering	$91,000	$64,000	$119,000
Chemical Engineering	$93,000	$66,000	$125,000
Metallurgical Engineering	$93,000	$66,000	$124,000
Petroleum Engineering	$129,000	$86,000	$210,000
Arts	$47,000	$33,000	$70,000
Studio Arts	$40,000	$28,000	$61,000
Visual and Performing Arts	$41,000	$29,000	$61,000
Drama and Theater Arts	$44,000	$31,000	$63,000
Music	$47,000	$34,000	$70,000
Fine Arts	$48,000	$32,000	$71,000
Commercial Art and Graphic Design	$50,000	$35,000	$73,000

Detailed Major	Annual Salary		
	50th percentile	25th percentile	75th percentile
Film Video and Photographic Arts	$50,000	$33,000	$73,000
Biology and Life Science	$55,000	$38,000	$81,000
Neuroscience	$47,000	$31,000	$78,000
Botany	$49,000	$32,000	$72,000
Ecology	$50,000	$33,000	$72,000
Molecular Biology	$52,000	$34,000	$74,000
Biology	$55,000	$38,000	$83,000
Environmental Science	$55,000	$40,000	$78,000
Miscellaneous Biology	$55,000	$37,000	$76,000
Zoology	$56,000	$37,000	$82,000
Biochemical Sciences	$57,000	$38,000	$86,000
Microbiology	$60,000	$41,000	$86,000
Business	$63,000	$42,000	$94,000
Hospitality Management	$51,000	$36,000	$75,000
Human Resources and Personnel Management	$57,000	$40,000	$83,000
Miscellaneous Business and Medical Administration	$57,000	$40,000	$88,000
International Business	$58,000	$41,000	$86,000
Business Management and Administration	$60,000	$41,000	$89,000
Marketing and Marketing Research	$62,000	$42,000	$94,000
General Business	$63,000	$42,000	$98,000
Accounting	$67,000	$45,000	$100,000
Operations Logistics and E-Commerce	$68,000	$49,000	$95,000
Finance	$70,000	$47,000	$105,000

Detailed Major	Annual Salary		
	50th percentile	25th percentile	75th percentile
Business Economics	$72,000	$50,000	$106,000
Management Information Systems and Statistics	$74,000	$52,000	$102,000
Communications and Journalism	$52,000	$38,000	$82,000
Communications and Mass Media	$52,000	$37,000	$82,000
Advertising and Public Relations	$52,000	$39,000	$79,000
Journalism	$54,000	$37,000	$83,000
Computers, Statistics, and Mathematics	$74,000	$50,000	$103,000
Miscellaneous Computer	$57,000	$40,000	$84,000
Computer and Information Systems	$67,000	$47,000	$92,000
Information Sciences	$70,000	$50,000	$96,000
Mathematics	$70,000	$45,000	$104,000
Statistics and Decision Science	$75,000	$49,000	$105,000
Applied Mathematics	$79,000	$52,000	$110,000
Computer Science	$80,000	$55,000	$109,000
Computer Engineering	$84,000	$62,000	$110,000
Education	$44,000	$34,000	$57,000
Early Childhood Education	$38,000	$30,000	$48,000
Teacher Education: Multiple Levels	$41,000	$32,000	$52,000
Elementary Education	$42,000	$33,000	$52,000
General Education	$44,000	$34,000	$59,000
Special Needs Education	$44,000	$36,000	$55,000

Detailed Major	Annual Salary		
	50th percentile	25th percentile	75th percentile
Language and Drama Education	$44,000	$35,000	$57,000
Art and Music Education	$44,000	$34,000	$57,000
Science and Computer Teacher Education	$46,000	$36,000	$60,000
Mathematics Teacher Education	$46,000	$37,000	$61,000
Social Science or History Teacher Education	$46,000	$35,000	$63,000
Secondary Teacher Education	$47,000	$37,000	$62,000
Physical and Health Education Teaching	$50,000	$37,000	$67,000
Miscellaneous Education	$51,000	$38,000	$73,000
Health	$63,000	$47,000	$84,000
Communication Disorders Sciences and Services	$44,000	$34,000	$62,000
Nutrition Sciences	$52,000	$36,000	$71,000
Health and Medical Preparatory Programs	$52,000	$37,000	$87,000
Health and Medical Administrative Services	$53,000	$38,000	$78,000
Miscellaneous Health Medical Professions	$55,000	$40,000	$75,000
Treatment Therapy Professions	$63,000	$42,000	$83,000
Nursing	$65,000	$50,000	$83,000
Pharmacy and Pharmaceutical Science and Administration	$110,000	$83,000	$126,000

Detailed Major	Annual Salary		
	50th percentile	25th percentile	75th percentile
Humanities and Liberal Arts	$50,000	$35,000	$75,000
Theology and Religious Vocations	$41,000	$29,000	$58,000
Multi/ Interdisciplinary Studies	$45,000	$36,000	$58,000
Composition and Speech	$46,000	$33,000	$71,000
Humanities	$47,000	$33,000	$70,000
Art History and Criticism	$47,000	$33,000	$73,000
Linguistics and Comparative Language and Literature	$49,000	$33,000	$73,000
Philosophy and Religious Studies	$49,000	$31,000	$73,000
Other Foreign Languages	$49,000	$33,000	$77,000
Area Ethnic and Civilization Studies	$50,000	$36,000	$76,000
Intercultural and International Studies	$51,000	$34,000	$74,000
French, German, Latin, and Other Common Foreign Language Studies	$51,000	$36,000	$73,000
English Language and Literature	$52,000	$36,000	$78,000
Liberal Arts	$52,000	$35,000	$76,000
History	$53,000	$37,000	$84,000
Industrial Arts, Consumer Services, and Recreation	$50,000	$36,000	$74,000
Family and Consumer Sciences	$43,000	$31,000	$62,000

Detailed Major	Annual Salary		
	50th percentile	25th percentile	75th percentile
Physical Fitness, Parks, Recreation, and Leisure	$47,000	$34,000	$65,000
Miscellaneous: Cosmetology, Construction, Repairs, and Production	$62,000	$41,000	$89,000
Transportation Sciences and Technologies	$70,000	$44,000	$100,000
Law and Public Policy	$53,000	$38,000	$77,000
Prelaw and Legal Studies	$50,000	$37,000	$71,000
Criminal Justice and Fire Protection	$53,000	$38,000	$77,000
Public Administration	$59,000	$41,000	$90,000
Public Policy	$63,000	$42,000	$94,000
Physical Sciences	$63,000	$42,000	$93,000
Multidisciplinary or General Science	$59,000	$40,000	$86,000
Physical Sciences	$60,000	$41,000	$84,000
Chemistry	$62,000	$42,000	$92,000
Geosciences	$62,000	$40,000	$89,000
Atmospheric Sciences and Meteorology	$63,000	$41,000	$95,000
Nuclear, Industrial Radiology, and Biological Technologies	$67,000	$49,000	$87,000
Geology and Earth Science	$68,000	$44,000	$100,000
Oceanography	$68,000	$45,000	$94,000
Physics	$77,000	$43,000	$113,000
Psychology and Social Work	$45,000	$33,000	$67,000
Human Services and Community Organization	$40,000	$30,000	$54,000

Detailed Major	Annual Salary		
	50th percentile	25th percentile	75th percentile
Social Work	$41,000	$31,000	$54,000
Psychology	$47,000	$34,000	$70,000
Social Psychology	$47,000	$36,000	$69,000
Industrial and Organizational Psychology	$65,000	$45,000	$88,000
Social Sciences	$58,000	$40,000	$92,000
Anthropology and Archeology	$47,000	$31,000	$72,000
Interdisciplinary Social Sciences	$47,000	$35,000	$68,000
Sociology	$49,000	$35,000	$72,000
General Social Sciences	$52,000	$36,000	$74,000
Criminology	$52,000	$37,000	$74,000
Miscellaneous Social Science	$54,000	$42,000	$84,000
Geography	$57,000	$41,000	$80,000
International Relations	$60,000	$41,000	$94,000
Political Science and Government	$62,000	$42,000	$96,000
Economics	$73,000	$46,000	$115,000

Notes

Chapter 1

3   **over \$1.6 trillion:** *Quarterly Report on Household Debt and Credit. 2020: Q2* (New York: Federal Reserve Bank of New York, 2020), https://www.newyorkfed.org/medialibrary/interactives/house holdcredit/data/pdf/hhdc_2020q2.pdf.

8   **decisions they'll later regret:** Rachel Fishman, *2015 College Decisions Survey: Part 1, Deciding to Go to College* (Washington, D.C.: New America Foundation, 2015), https://static.newamerica.org/attachments/3248-deciding-to-go-to-college/CollegeDecisions_PartI.148dcab30a0e414ea2a52f0d8fb04e7b.pdf.

9   **The median household in the United States:** Jessica Semega, Melissa Kollar, Emily A. Shrider, and John F. Creamer, *Income and Poverty in the United States: 2019* (Washington, D.C.: US Census Bureau, 2020), https://www.census.gov/content/dam/Census/library/publications/2020/demo/p60-270.pdf.

9   **annual earnings of approximately \$50,000:** *NACE Salary Survey* (Bethlehem, PA: National Association of Colleges and Employers, 2019), https://www.naceweb.org/uploadedfiles/files/2019/publication/executive-summary/2019-nace-salary-survey-summer-executive-summary.pdf.

10   **the return you'd expect:** Jaison R. Abel and Richard Deitz, "Despite Rising Costs, College Is Still a Good Investment," *Liberty Street Economics* (blog), Federal Reserve Bank of New York, last modified

June 5, 2019, https://libertystreeteconomics.newyorkfed.org/
2019/06/despite-rising-costs-college-is-still-a-good-investment
.html.

10 **Georgetown University recently published:** Anthony P. Carnevale, Ban Cheah, and Martin Van Der Werf, *A First Try at ROI:
Ranking 4,500 Colleges* (Washington, D.C.: Georgetown University
Center on Education and the Workforce, 2020), https://1gyhoq
479ufd3yna29x7ubjn-wpengine.netdna-ssl.com/wp-content/
uploads/College_ROI.pdf.

11 **for their bachelor's degree:** Beth Akers, Kim Dancy, and Jason
Delisle, *College Affordability Update: Value, Price, and Choice in U.S.
Higher Education* (New York: Manhattan Institute, 2019), https://
www.manhattan-institute.org/college-affordability-update.

12 **just over $15,000 (including living expenses):** Jennifer Ma,
Sandy Baum, Matea Pender, and C. J. Libassi, *Trends in College Pricing
2019* (New York: College Board, 2019), https://research.college
board.org/pdf/trends-college-pricing-2019-full-report.pdf.

12 **north of 12 percent:** Alina Comoreanu, *Credit Card Landscape Report* (Washington, D.C.: WalletHub, 2020), https://wallethub.com/
edu/cc/credit-card-landscape-report/24927/#interest-rates.

14 **with incomes below $30,000:** Akers, Dancy, and Delisle, *College
Affordability Update.*

14 **$1 million in student debt:** Josh Mitchell, "Mike Meru Has
$1 Million in Student Loans. How Did That Happen?," *The Wall
Street Journal,* May 25, 2018, https://www.wsj.com/articles/mike
-meru-has-1-million-in-student-loans-how-did-that-happen-15272
52975.

14 **balance at graduation:** Ma et al., *Trends in College Pricing 2019.*

14 **median earnings for that college-educated millennial:** "PINC-
03: Educational Attainment—People 25 Years Old and Over, by
Total Money Earnings, Work Experience, Age, Race, Hispanic
Origin, and Sex," tables, US Census Bureau, 2020, https://www
.census.gov/data/tables/time-series/demo/income-poverty/
cps-pinc/pinc-03.html.

14 **on monthly car payments:** "Consumer Expenditure Surveys,"

CE Tables, US Bureau of Labor Statistics, last modified September 22, 2020, https://www.bls.gov/cex/tables.htm#annual.

15 **millennials with master's and professional degrees:** "PINC-03."

15 **who often didn't complete a degree:** Sandy Baum, Jennifer Ma, Matea Pender, and C. J. Libassi, *Trends in Student Aid 2019* (New York: College Board, 2019), https://research.collegeboard.org/pdf/trends-student-aid-2019-full-report.pdf.

Chapter 2

19 **over the course of their lifetime:** Douglas Webber, *Is College Worth It? Going Beyond Averages* (Washington, D.C.: Third Way, 2018), https://www.thirdway.org/report/is-college-worth-it-going-beyond-averages.

22 **or others' performance:** Scott Plous, *The Psychology of Judgment and Decision Making* (New York: McGraw-Hill, 1993).

24 **can often be mitigated or avoided:** National Center for Education Statistics, *Baccalaureate and Beyond (B&B:16/17): A First Look at the Employment and Educational Experiences of College Graduates, 1 Year Later* (Washington, D.C.: US Department of Education, 2020).

25 **in four years or less:** National Center for Education Statistics, *Integrated Postsecondary Education Data System (IPEDS)* (Washington, D.C.: US Department of Education, 2018).

25 **aren't enrolled full-time:** Table 303.10, Digest of Education Statistics, National Center for Education Statistics, accessed September 23, 2020, https://nces.ed.gov/programs/digest/d18/tables/dt18_303.50.asp.

27 **top motivation for enrolling in college:** Rachel Fishman, *2015 College Decisions Survey: Part 1, Deciding to Go to College* (Washington, D.C.: New America Foundation, 2015), https://static.newamerica.org/attachments/3248-deciding-to-go-to-college/CollegeDecisions_PartI.148dcab30a0e414ea2a52f0d8fb04e7b.pdf.

27 **average earnings for graduates:** "The Best Colleges in America, Ranked by Value," Best Colleges 2020, Money.com, last modified August 25, 2020, https://money.com/best-college.

28 **the value in different options:** "Best Value Colleges," PayScale, accessed September 22, 2020, https://www.payscale.com/college-roi.

30 **Harvard's graduate theater program:** "Debt to Earnings Data Spreadsheet: GE-DMYR-2015-Final-Rates.xls," Federal Student Aid, US Department of Education, accessed September 22, 2020, https://studentaid.gov/sites/default/files/GE-DMYR-2015-Final-Rates.xls.

30 **graduates in their top field of study:** "DigiPen Institute of Technology," College Scorecard, US Department of Education, accessed September 23, 2020, https://collegescorecard.ed.gov/school/?443410-DigiPen-Institute-of-Technology.

32 **more than the theology major:** Douglas A. Webber, "Projected Lifetime Earnings by Major," Doug-Webber.com, last modified December 1, 2019, http://www.doug-webber.com/expected_all.pdf.

35 **the practice of radiology:** Michael Walter, "If You Think AI Will Never Replace Radiologists—You May Want to Think Again," *Radiology Business,* May 14, 2018, https://www.radiologybusiness.com/topics/artificial-intelligence/if-you-think-ai-will-never-replace-radiologists-you-may-want-think.

Chapter 3

41 **argument of "academic deference":** Academic deference flows from the First Amendment, which our courts hold sacrosanct. This unique position of institutions of higher education is due to their general embrace of free speech and academic independence as a core value rather than to an explicit belief that institutions of higher education are above the law.

42 **borrowed while they were enrolled:** Libby Nelson, "Indiana University Used This One Weird Trick to Cut Student Debt," *Vox,* July 26, 2015, https://www.vox.com/2015/7/26/9041283/indiana-university-debt-letters.

44 **didn't have any student debt at all:** Elizabeth Akers and Matthew Chingos, *Are College Students Borrowing Blindly?* (Washington, D.C.: Brookings Institution, 2014), https://www.brookings.edu/wp-content/uploads/2016/06/Are-College-Students-Borrowing-Blindly_Dec-2014.pdf.

50 **where to go and how much to pay:** Michael D. Shear, "With Website to Research Colleges, Obama Abandons Ranking System," *New York Times*, September 12, 2015, https://www.nytimes.com/2015/09/13/us/with-website-to-research-colleges-obama-abandons-ranking-system.html.

56 **public nonflagship colleges:** Rajashra Chakrabarti, Michael Lovenhein, and Kevin Morris, "The Changing Higher Education Landscape," *Liberty Street Economics* (blog), September 6, 2016, https://libertystreeteconomics.newyorkfed.org/2016/09/the-changing-higher-education-landscape.html#.V9AYhj4rKCd.

57 **paying back their loans in the same year:** Adam Looney and Constantine Yannelis, *A Crisis in Student Loans? How Changes in the Characteristics of Borrowers and the Institutions They Attended Contributed to Rising Loan Defaults* (Washington, D.C.: Brookings Institution, 2015), https://www.brookings.edu/bpea-articles/a-crisis-in-student-loans-how-changes-in-the-characteristics-of-borrowers-and-in-the-institutions-they-attended-contributed-to-rising-loan-defaults.

57 **the Gainful Employment Regulations:** The explicit rationale for the Gainful Employment Regulations was to put in place higher standards for programs of study that aimed specifically to place graduates in a certain profession. Because career training programs are disproportionately administered by for-profit colleges, the introduction of these regulations is often interpreted as an attempt to hold for-profit colleges to a different standard.

Chapter 4

63 **three more years at Ithaca:** To be clear, there is nothing inherently wrong with Ithaca College. In fact, graduates from SUNY

Albany and Ithaca College earn a nearly identical range of salaries after graduation, and they graduate at coincidentally similar rates. For others on a different path or with different preferences, Ithaca College may be a perfect fit both financially and in terms of the opportunities it provides.

63   **at the time they leave high school:** Liz Freedman, "The Developmental Disconnect in Choosing a Major: Why Institutions Should Prohibit Choice until Second Year," *The Mentor* 15 (2013), https://journals.psu.edu/mentor/article/view/61278/60911.

65   **graduates from Harvard University:** "Salaries for Harvard University Graduates," PayScale, accessed September 23, 2020, https://www.payscale.com/research/US/School=Harvard_University/Salary.

65   **across all four-year colleges:** Stephen Miller, "Average Starting Salaries for Recent College Grads Hovers near $51,000," Society for Human Resource Management, August 22, 2019, https://www.shrm.org/resourcesandtools/hr-topics/compensation/pages/average-starting-salary-for-recent-college-grads.aspx.

65   **the same (or very similar) price tags:** "Harvard University," College Scorecard, US Department of Education, accessed September 23, 2020, https://collegescorecard.ed.gov/school/?166027-Harvard-University.

65   **tuition, fees, and textbooks:** "University of Central Florida," College Navigator, National Center for Education Statistics, Institute for Education Sciences, accessed September 23, 2020, https://nces.ed.gov/collegenavigator/?q=university+of+central+florida&s=all&id=132903#expenses.

66   **approximately $23,000 annually:** Jennifer Ma, Matea Pender, and Meredith Welch, *Education Pays 2019: The Benefits of Higher Education for Individuals and Society* (Washington, D.C.: College Board, 2019), https://research.collegeboard.org/pdf/education-pays–2019-full-report.pdf.

66   **early-career UCF graduates:** "Salaries for University of Central Florida (UCF) Graduates," PayScale, accessed September 23, 2020, https://www.payscale.com/research/US/School=University_of_Central_Florida_(UCF)/Salary.

71   **Georgetown University Center on Education and the Work-force:** Anthony P. Carnevale, Ban Cheah, and Martin Van Der Werf, *The Economic Value of College Majors* (Washington, D.C.: Georgetown University Center on Education and the Workforce, 2015), https://1gyhoq479ufd3yna29x7ubjn-wpengine.netdna-ssl .com/wp-content/uploads/The-Economic-Value-of-College -Majors-Full-Report-web-FINAL.pdf.

Chapter 5

75   **In 2014, researchers from:** Matt McDonald and Pat Brady, "The Plural of Anecdote is Data (Except for Student Loan Debt)" Hamilton Place Strategies, accessed November 6, 2020, https://www .consumerfinancemonitor.com/wp-content/uploads/sites/ 14/2014/08/Media-coverage-of-student-debt_1.pdf.

75   **typical student loan borrowers:** Beth Akers and Matthew Chingos, *Game of Loans: Reconciling the Rhetoric and Reality of Student Debt* (Princeton, N.J.: Princeton University Press, 2018).

86   **people who didn't borrow:** Beth Akers, "Reconsidering the Conventional Wisdom on Student Loan Debt and Home Owner-ship," Brookings Institution, May 8, 2020, https://www.brookings .edu/research/reconsidering-the-conventional-wisdom-on -student-loan-debt-and-home-ownership/.

89   **when I read about one study:** Stephen Burd and Rachel Fish-man, *Decoding the Cost of College: The Case for Transparent Financial Aid Letters* (Washington, D.C.: New America, 2018), https://d1y8sb8igg 2f8e.cloudfront.net/documents/Decoding_the_Cost_of_College _Final_6218.pdf.

91   **maximum award amount was capped:** "Federal Pell Grants," Federal Student Aid, US Department of Education, accessed September 22, 2020, https://studentaid.gov/understand-aid/types/ grants/pell.

93   **unwittingly reduced their chances of graduating:** Sarah R. Cohodes and Joshua S. Goodman, "Merit Aid, College Quality, and College Completion: Massachusetts' Adams Scholarship as an

In-Kind Subsidy," *American Economic Journal: Applied Economics* 6, no. 4 (2014): 251–85.

95   **during his time in office:** William J. Bennett, "Our Greedy Colleges," *The New York Times,* February 18, 1987, https://www .nytimes.com/1987/02/18/opinion/our-greedy-colleges.html.

Chapter 6

98   **Soccer star David Beckham:** Luke Graham, "10 Expensively Insured Body Parts," CNBC, September 9, 2016, https://www .cnbc.com/2016/09/09/10-expensively-insured-body-parts .html.

102   **a full ten years after graduation:** "Adrian College," College Scorecard, US Department of Education, accessed September 23, 2020, https://collegescorecard.ed.gov/school/?168528 -Adrian-College.

103   **guaranteeing money back:** Adrian College no longer offers the repayment assistance program. I presume they have simply moved on to other initiatives to promote enrollment.

104   **coding boot camps like Flatiron School:** "Money-Back Guarantee for Qualifying Programs," Flatiron School, accessed September 23, 2020, https://flatironschool.com/career-services -commitment.

104   **Thomas College in Maine:** "Guaranteed Job Program™," Thomas College, accessed September 23, 2020, https://www .thomas.edu/guarantees/.

105   **others, such as Davenport University:** "Employment Guarantee," Davenport University, accessed September 23, 2020, https:// www.davenport.edu/employment-guarantee.

107   **off the hook completely:** By current tax law, debt forgiveness is considered taxable income. It seems likely to me that this will change as more borrowers reach forgiveness and policy makers are pressured to eliminate this additional economic burden.

107 **in twenty years:** Borrowers who work in public service are eligible to have loans forgiven after ten years.

107 **confidence about their future job prospects:** Beth Akers, *Should College Come with a Money-Back Guarantee?* (New York: Manhattan Institute, 2019), https://www.manhattan-institute.org/college-money-back-guarantee-student-loans.

Chapter 7

116 **mastering a skill or subject:** Caren Arbeit, Alexander Bentz, Emily Forrest Cataldi, and Herschel Sanders, *Alternative and Independent: The Universe of Technology-Related "Bootcamps"* (Research Triangle Park, NC: RTI International, 2019), https://www.rti.org/rti-press-publication/alternative-and-independent.

116 **landing students in high-paying jobs:** Steve Lohr, "As Tech Booms, Workers Turn to Coding for Career Change," *New York Times,* July 28, 2015, https://www.nytimes.com/2015/07/29/technology/code-academy-as-career-game-changer.html.

116 **lasts an average of fourteen weeks:** Liz Eggleston, *The Growth of Coding Bootcamps 2018* (New York: Course Report, 2018), https://www.coursereport.com/reports/2018-coding-bootcamp-market-size-research.

121 **a monthly living stipend of $2,500:** Allison Dulin Salisbury, "New Higher-Ed Business Models That Millions of Americans Need to Get Better Jobs," *EdSurge,* April 1, 2019, https://www.edsurge.com/news/2019-04-01-new-higher-ed-business-models-millions-of-americans-need-to-get-better-jobs.

122 **difficulty recruiting suitable job candidates:** "The Skills Gap 2019," Society of Human Resource Managers, February 5, 2019, https://www.shrm.org/hr-today/trends-and-forecasting/research-and-surveys/pages/skills-gap-2019.aspx.

122 **seven million unfilled jobs in the US economy:** "Job Openings and Labor Turnover Summary," Economic News Release, US Bureau of Labor Statistics, last modified September 9, 2020, https://www.bls.gov/news.release/pdf/jolts.pdf.

123 **the diversity of Americans who could benefit:** "Apprenticeship in Review," Center on Education and Labor, New America,
last modified November 11, 2019, https://www.newamerica.org/
education-policy/reports/apprenticeship-review/apprenticeship
-in-review-2018.

Index

About the Author

Beth Akers is a senior fellow at the Manhattan Institute, where her work focuses on labor economics and the economics of higher education. Previously, she was a fellow at the Brookings Institution and a staff economist with the Council of Economic Advisers under President George W. Bush.

Akers has previously coauthored *Game of Loans: The Rhetoric and Reality of Student Debt*. Her writing and research have been featured in, among others, *The New York Times*, *USA Today*, *The Wall Street Journal*, *The Washington Post*, Bloomberg, Quartz, *Newsweek*, and *The Hill*. She has appeared on CNBC, ABC News, Bloomberg TV, and C-SPAN, among other TV and radio networks.

Akers received a BS in mathematics and economics from SUNY Albany and a PhD in economics from Columbia University.

She lives in Salt Lake City, Utah, with her husband and son and spends much of her free time adventuring in the mountains.

About the Type

This book was set in Albertina, a typeface created by Dutch calligrapher and designer Chris Brand (1921–98). Brand's original drawings, based on calligraphic principles, were modified considerably to conform to the technological limitations of typesetting in the early 1960s. The development of digital technology later allowed Frank E. Blokland (b. 1959) of the Dutch Type Library to restore the typeface to its creator's original intentions.